Like friendly
Kari walk you
Blessing. When the cry of the past bullies again with "not
enough," "unlovable," "broken," "stuck," or "alone," *Your
Journey from Broken to Blessed* stands beside you, guiding
the way forward to healing, hope, and the real joy you
crave! I devoured this book in one sitting and am going
back to linger in the pages. Grab a copy for yourself, and
send one to a friend!

    DIANA MESCHER, Bible study teacher and speaker

We were created in, through, and for relationship, not
only with God but also with one another. *Your Journey
from Broken to Blessed* beautifully captures God's heartbeat
for us to feel loved and secure. Dr. Trent and his daughter
Kari walk this pathway with transparency and biblical
truth to a destination full of hope and blessing.

    DR. ERIC SCALISE, president of Hope for the Heart

After the transformative gift of *The Blessing*, Dr. John
Trent now joins with his daughter Kari Trent Stageberg to
address the deeply felt pain of those who never received
the Blessing they longed for. *Your Journey from Broken to
Blessed* is a lifeline of hope, offering biblically grounded,
practical steps for healing and restoration. With profound
empathy and personal insight, this book invites readers
to move from heartache to healing, from brokenness to
blessing. It's a must-read for anyone yearning to break free
from the past and embrace the love, purpose, and hope
God has for them. I highly recommend it.

    JIM McGUIRE, founder of THRYVE Leaders

In *Your Journey from Broken to Blessed: Finding the Love You Didn't Receive*, John and Kari remind us that hope is never lost when we place Jesus at the center of our lives. Having many times witnessed firsthand the transformative power of a blessing, I wholeheartedly recommend this book to the broken, the restored, and those rejoicing in their journey.

JOE PELLEGRINO, president of Legacy Minded Men

In *Your Journey from Broken to Blessed*, Dr. John Trent and Kari Trent Stageberg bring hope and a way home for the reader, regardless of the pain endured in your family of origin or adult relationships.

Their statement "In truth, way down to the very cells in our bodies, *we can reverse the curse.* We can move past having someone fail to be emotionally or physically present in our pasts—the people who chose to subtract from our lives" offers hope to countless people who have erroneously concluded, *I can never heal from the pain, abuse, neglect, and/or abandonment I have experienced.*

This book indeed offers a road map for your journey from hurt to freedom, hope, and blessing. God is able, and God will make a way, yet it starts with each of us being willing to surrender and make a choice. Picking up this book is not for the faint of heart, yet with courage and biblical truth, you will be given an incredible opportunity to join with God in giving you the freedom you have desired for years. We couldn't endorse this book with more passion than we are. Well done, John and Kari: This is perhaps your greatest work.

DR. GARY AND BARB ROSBERG, America's Family Coaches, authors, radio broadcasters, podcasters, and speakers

Dr. John Trent and Kari Trent Stageberg offer a timely guide for those who missed out on a blessing from an earthly father. Their practical insights shed light on how to overcome the crippling feeling of being unaccepted and unacceptable. Their words will encourage you and empower you to experience the unparalleled power of the Blessing.

REV. JOSHUA R. SHERRARD, chair of the Sherrard Institute and president and CEO of Strategic Navigators, Inc.

For those of you seeking healing and freedom from the brokenness in your life, this book provides a clear path to healing and freedom. *Your Journey from Broken to Blessed* gives us hope and provides a clear, practical path to healing and freedom in our hearts and in our homes. This book is for anyone who wants to know how to change their life and family—from broken to blessed.

SUSAN SOWELL, adult discipleship minister at Kingsland Baptist Church

In *Your Journey from Broken to Blessed*, Dr. John Trent guides readers through a process that begins with recognizing the absence of the Blessing in their lives and starts them on a journey of healing. By exploring the five key elements of the Blessing, readers are led through the process of rebuilding their emotional and spiritual well-being, which helps them move from pain and longing to restoration and empowerment. The true power of *Your Journey from Broken to Blessed* lies in its ability to help individuals get to a place of passing the Blessing on to others, creating a cycle of love and healing.

JEFF THIBAULT, president of Parenting Special Kids Network

A Focus on the Family resource
published by Tyndale House Publishers

JOHN TRENT, Ph.D.
KARI TRENT STAGEBERG

YOUR JOURNEY

FROM

BROKEN

TO

BLESSED

Finding the Love
You Didn't Receive

To Doug Barram, who first showed me a picture of Jesus' love.
To Mike Burnidge, whose lifelong friendship
and smile were constant gifts from God.
To my precious wife, Cindy, who pictures every
day what I prayed for in a godly wife.
And in special memory of my mother, Zoa, who filled
my life with boxes full of loving snapshots.
I love you, Mom.

JOHN TRENT

To the three men in my life whom I get to bless and
do life with: my husband, Joey, and two wonderful
young men, Lincoln and Sawyer. And to my beloved
mom, dad, and sister, Laura, who chose to bless me and
have kept blessing me all through my journey.

KARI TRENT STAGEBERG

Contents

A single picture has the power to stop us in our tracks and reveal to us just who we are.

MARVIN HEIFERMAN AND CAROLE KISMARIC,
Talking Pictures: People Speak about the Photographs That Speak to Them

CHAPTER 1

IN SEARCH OF
THE BLESSING

Emma looked out over the darkly dressed crowd packed like sardines into every nook and cranny of the small church. She stalled for time as she adjusted the microphone on the podium and glanced down at the note card in her hand.

Could she really read what she had written?

Clearing her throat, she began, "My dad was . . ." But the rest of the words stuck in her throat.

Her dad was abusive. Her dad was a drunk. Her dad was mean, angry, and horrible to Emma, her mother, and her sisters. Her dad had single-handedly ruined her childhood. He'd done his best to ruin her adult life too. Her dad had never told her he loved her or said he was proud of her. And he never thought anything she did was good enough.

She had spent her entire life trying to get away from his abuse, and now that his life had ended, she was more than a little angry that she was supposed to put the truth of who he was to the side and say positive and loving things about a man who had made her life a living nightmare.

All those supposed positives were neatly laid out on the note card she held. Words that were essentially lies about what a great man her father had been and how well he had loved her and his family.

To the outside world, her dad fit the picture of a loving father and husband. He was active in church, served on multiple non-profit boards, ran a successful business, and was adored in her small town due to being a high school football legend turned winning high school football coach.

But none of them saw what had happened behind closed doors. None of them knew the pain and destruction he had caused. And now that he was dead, none of them knew the loss she was feeling over the fact that things were final. Her father would never change. He would never tell her he loved her. He would never think his oldest daughter was good enough. Their relationship would never be repaired.

Emma looked up and locked eyes with her mom and two sisters. And in that moment, it was as if everything she had been battling finally came to a head. She knew that if she went along with the lie here, she would continue to go along with it the rest of her life. And in that moment, she realized it was time to make a choice.

So she did something that shocked even her. She shook her head, embraced every emotion that coursed through her body, and walked silently off the stage.

To everyone in the church, it appeared as though the loss of her father was too hard for her to talk about. She was met with sympathy and kindness. But for Emma, it was much more significant.

She had finally made a life-changing decision. She was no longer going to lie about or cover up what had happened. She was going to heal and move forward, no matter what it took. She was determined to no longer be stuck in the darkness and brokenness her father had left behind.

What Emma didn't realize was that she was about to discover the healing tool she needed—one that would help her, her mother, and her sisters. Emma was about to discover the Blessing. And on a deeper level, she would answer:

What if I never got the Blessing?

Your story may not look exactly like Emma's, but many of us find ourselves—regardless of our age, stage of life, or successes—asking the same questions. *Am I really loved? Am I really enough? Do I really matter? Why didn't he want me? Why didn't she love me? Why could I never measure up?*

Those of us facing these questions are often missing what we and the Bible call *the Blessing*.

But what is the Blessing? And how can it help you, Emma, and others heal and find solid, life-giving answers to the questions above?

Let me (John) describe where my story of the Blessing began. Then we'll move forward to *your* story of blessing.

The Night I First Saw the Blessing

More than forty years ago, I was an intern at a psychiatric hospital in Richardson, Texas. There I would hear a daily dose of broken dreams and shattered hearts as a part of each shift.

That's also when an incredible thing happened in my life.

I was at home. It was late on a Saturday night. I was gathering my notes, preparing to teach a Bible study for a couples' class my wife and I led at our church. We were going through the book of Genesis, and it was time to teach on chapter 27.

I'd read the story there before and heard it talked about numerous times, though never from a relational perspective. That night, it was as if the Lord took scales off my eyes and gave me a picture of something I'd never really seen before.

It was a picture of twin brothers, Jacob and Esau. I could relate because I'm a twin. And in this story, the brothers were desperately struggling to get the same thing.

They were both in search of their father's blessing.

That night, it was as if *I* were standing inside their father Isaac's tent.

I could see Esau's eyes light up when he heard that at long last it was time to receive his father's blessing. His excitement radiated as he ran out to hunt, field dress, and cook the meal that would signal his time of blessing.

That night, it was as if the Lord took scales off my eyes and gave me a picture of something I'd never really seen before.

I saw Rebekah gather her robes and run through the hot sand, grabbing Jacob, her favorite son. Furiously they invented a plan to deceive his father.

I could smell the meal that mother and younger son cooked up. And picture how Jacob brought it to his father.

Their plan almost failed because Isaac was doubtful and full of questions. ("How is it that you have it so quickly?" [Genesis 27:20] and "Are you really my son Esau?" [Genesis 27:24].) But then those questions gave way to Jacob receiving a wonderful blessing.

Then I saw Jacob go out one side of the tent, filled with joy. And at almost the same moment, I saw his brother rush in the other side with his own savory offering for his father.

Esau's face was lit with expectation.

"Let my father arise and eat of his son's game, that you may bless me" (Genesis 27:31).

His smile nearly split his face as he asked for his blessing.

But then his heart dropped. For he heard there would be no blessing.

His smile turned into a look of shock, then disbelief, and finally rage as the reality that he would never receive his father's blessing washed over him.

I saw all this in that snapshot of the Scriptures because I realized I was seeing it each day in the psychiatric hospital. But I also realized I had *lived* it in many ways over many years with my own father.

I had been carrying Esau's heart-wrenching cry, "Bless me, me as well, my father!" (Genesis 27:34), in my heart of hearts since I was a child.

The concept of the Blessing suddenly exploded before me like the very end of a massive fireworks show.

There it was! A biblical way of looking at my life that answered many of my inner struggles. Before that night, I'd had no name for it. Now I did.

My father had left my mother, my two brothers, and me when I was two months old. He never came back. I didn't know him. But it was my father's blessing I had sought a hundred times and more. I had longed for it. Lived for it for years. And yet it always remained just out of reach.

Esau's cry was not just an echo of my own heartache. It went to the heart of the life stories I was hearing every day in the psychiatric hospital. I knew now what many of them were struggling with. Men and women were saying, *crying, begging* in their brokenness, "Bless me, Mom. Bless me, Dad. Please!"

Have you ever said, out loud or in your heart, words like that? It's a cry to be seen and valued, loved and cared for, blessed and not cursed. Perhaps, like Emma, you have a hole in your soul so deep that no accomplishment or relationship can seem to fill it. *If so, this book is for you.*

What If I Missed the Blessing?

If this term, *the Blessing*, is new to you, this book will provide a powerful introduction to what the Blessing is and means—how important it can be in your life and with those you love.[1] But after decades of helping people give and live the Blessing, we turn our focus here to the thousands more whose cry growing up echoed Esau's cry of loss.

"Bless me, me as well!"

Our cry arises because that significant person in our lives, for whatever reason, made a choice *not* to bless us. All parents make a choice, even if they're not aware they're making it, to bless or not to bless a child. And if we missed the Blessing, there follows a cascade of questions like these:

- *What was wrong with me?*
- *Why did my sibling receive it . . . but I didn't?*
- *Why now, after so many years, do I still feel so incomplete and downhearted about missing it?*

This is a book for those of us who grew up without the Blessing. It's also for those of us who have experienced trauma, loss, and pain that has done its best to erase any form of blessing we've received.

This book is for those of us who struggled (and still struggle) with feeling unloved or unwanted. Many of us were cut off from one or even both parents by divorce, circumstance, or choice. We are men and women who, even today, often experience a deep sense of loneliness in a crowd. We can struggle in making close friendships or relating well with others. And we can fight with psychosomatic or genuine physical symptoms from anxiety, fear, or depression. For, as we'll see, *if we miss the Blessing, our minds, hearts, and bodies keep score.*

If we miss the Blessing, our minds, hearts, and bodies keep score.

Missing and searching for a lost blessing can leave us with a lifelong, nagging sense of insecurity. While not formally named as a psychological ailment or affliction (though we believe it should be), the lack of a parent's blessing is undeniably real. It's often at the heart of why we struggle with depression. It can be the genesis of why we still feel so empty, no matter what award or success we've gained.

But all that hurt doesn't have to be our end or our only choice in life.

In truth, way down to the very cells in our bodies, *we can reverse the curse.* We can move past having someone fail to be emotionally or physically present in our pasts—the people who chose to subtract from our lives (see Deuteronomy 23:5).

But, perhaps even more important, we can learn to be people who receive, give, and live the Blessing. We can, with God's help and strength, move past the negative pictures that haunt us and so change not only our stories but also the stories of generations that follow.

We can come face-to-face with our fears and hurts. We'll even see in the miraculous way God has wired us neurologically that *we can rewire our brains* with missing words of blessing! You'll receive those words of blessing in this book.

We can move from a frozen, yearslong *missing-blessing mindset* to one of being able to receive the Blessing and become people of blessing ourselves!

If it is true that photographic images have changed our lives,
we wanted to know why. How have photographs shaped
our personal histories and our collective imagination?
How do we read pictures? What do we read into them?

MARVIN HEIFERMAN AND CAROL KISMARIC,
Talking Pictures: People Speak about the Photographs That Speak to Them

CHAPTER 2

YOUR JOURNEY FROM HURT TO FREEDOM, HOPE, AND BLESSING

When we last saw Emma, she had walked off the stage at her father's funeral, determined to find a way to heal from the pain in her past. Not long after that, Emma began to walk down a path of healing, restoration, and blessing. It's the very path we're excited to share with you in this book.

However, the first step on that journey is a choice. Emma made it standing on the stage at her father's funeral. And we're going to ask you to make it right now, wherever you are. It's time to make the choice to truly trust the Lord with the pictures of your life story. Every picture. Even the painful, hidden, shameful ones. Or the ones you've tried to hide away.

I (Kari) deeply understand that this may not be an easy choice to make. While I was blessed to grow up in a home full of the Blessing, I found myself in an abusive relationship in my early twenties. It would leave me broken emotionally and physically. As a domestic-violence survivor, I've got many painful pictures. They bring back words, fear, emotions, and shame. They've told me again and again that I don't matter. That I'll never be enough. That God isn't really capable of healing *that*. That I'm unloved. Unworthy. And that I'll never be free from what was said or what happened.

Or maybe (like me, Kari) you've made decisions you're not proud of. Decisions that have hurt those you love and made you question your very identity. Maybe those decisions have built layers of guilt, shame, and brokenness that you feel no amount of grace could ever fully cover.

But here's the truth and the reason we're asking you to start by making such a big decision: *God is able.* He's able to heal. He's able to redeem. He's able to restore. Nothing we've done, or that has been done to us, can separate us from His love (see Romans 8:38-39).

God is also kind. He's gentle with our hearts and our healing. However, to really heal, to really allow Him to do what only He can do and turn ashes into beauty, we have to allow Him to hold our pain. Give Him access to those memories. Let Him see the pictures we'd rather hide away. Yes, He already knows them. But healing comes when we trust God with our pain, sin, and brokenness and allow Him to walk us through those moments. Then we can experience His love, acceptance, and strength as He turns our deepest pain into healing, grace, and redemption.

So wherever you are right now, please say these words with us: "Lord, I'm ready to make the choice to give You access to every picture of my life story. I'm ready to heal. I'm ready to trust You. I know You won't leave me in the middle of the mess or destroyed by the pain. And I trust that You're doing a new thing. You're able. And You are turning brokenness into blessing."

Pictures Are Powerful

Now that you've made that empowering choice, let's talk about why those pictures we've mentioned are so powerful when it comes to the Blessing and our own healing.

The heart remembers the words, the pictures, and the moments when we realized we did or didn't receive the Blessing. In many ways, the heart is like the online storage drive where we keep the photographs we've taken—that drive we haven't had the time to sort through and organize.

Day after day, week after week, year after year, pictures are dropped into that drive. Pictures of birthdays. Christmas mornings. The first Little League game or soccer practice. The first and only piano recital. The last-day-of-school party. The most exhilarating moment. The most embarrassing one. The overexposed. The underexposed. The ones where the flash didn't go off. The faded. The blurred. The stories of our lives.

If we missed the Blessing and we want to heal personally and bless others, we must understand the sources that have shaped our lives.

By the time we reach adulthood, the drive is bulging with memories. We take those memories with us everywhere we go. Memories of a parent's smile . . . or scowl. Memories of a teacher's praise . . . or ridicule. Memories of a classmate's kindness . . . or cruelty.

Pictures that carry a blessing . . . or convey a curse.

If we missed the Blessing, there's tremendous power in those negative pictures. They can push us down, defeat us, and continue to discourage us even now, perhaps decades after we've moved across the street or across the country to get away from those pictures.

But know this: If we missed the Blessing and we want to heal personally and bless others, we must understand the sources that have shaped our lives.

Did we receive love, affirmation, and encouragement? Was there the kind of support in our pasts that filled and lifted our hearts and minds? Were there people who acted like locks in a river and helped raise us up and move us forward? Or were our pasts full of those who were like anchors, full of words and actions that brought us down and kept us stuck?

We may want to bless someone with a positive future (one of the elements of the Blessing, as we'll see). But we'll often fail if we don't believe we have a special future ourselves. So our blessing becomes paper-thin and tears into pieces when we try to hand it off to another.

We want you to see in our error-filled lives (as well as in the priceless, unfailing pictures from Scripture) that water *can* rise above its source. That the love of God, expressed in His only Son, can lift up your head, pull you out of the mud, and wash away feelings of shame and hopelessness.

Because of Him, you are wanted, redeemed, loved, and full of great value.

Because of Him, you can become a person who blesses others.

Even if you've never received the Blessing yourself.

The Journey Begins: From Missing to Living the Blessing

We pray that in reading this book you'll experience some specific, meaningful, emotionally and spiritually grounding *moments*. Perhaps they will happen as you read a story or quote. Or God will use a specific Scripture to grab your heart. More likely, they will come when you're out jogging or walking after having read something. Suddenly a thought or insight will pop into your mind that makes total sense.

In clinical language, this is called *second-order change*, as opposed to *first-order change*. First-order change is just more of the same. Think about having a bad dream. Now just run faster to get away. There's no real change. You're still stuck inside that bad dream.

Second-order change happens when something or someone *outside us*—like the alarm clock, the dog barking, your child crying out, or God's Word and Spirit—*breaks in from the outside and wakes us up*. It's that moment when you go from bad dream to fully awake and fully alive.

In missing the Blessing, life can become a lot like a terrible dream lived over and over. Or, more poetically, remember how C. S. Lewis depicted a land where it's always winter but never Christmas. Only it's real life to us.

If that never-Christmas-never-spring experience was your life growing up, we pray that this book will wake you up from the effects of having missed the Blessing. We pray the Lord will use His Word, this book, and the memories and insights you will generate to wake you up and embolden you to finally make the changes you can make. Our hope is that, now or a month from now, you will be convinced that you can gain and give and live the Blessing—even if you never received it!

How can that happen?

Let's check in with Emma and summarize her journey as we outline the path we'll be taking in the chapters that follow.

The Path We'll Follow

Three weeks after Emma walked off the stage at her father's funeral, she found herself sitting in her counselor's office. It was their second session in as many weeks, and Emma had just finished providing the background of her story and what had led her to seek extra help.

After hearing Emma's story, her counselor gave her a book to read for homework. It was the book we wrote with Gary Smalley, *The Blessing*.

Over the next few weeks, Emma read through the book and discovered not only a name for what she had been missing but also an outline for healing.

As she learned more about the Blessing and how its absence shaped her life story, she began to heal. That healing led to receiving God's blessing. Then to forgiving her father. And eventually to being able to bless her mom, sisters, and other family members who were still broken and hurting from her father's abuse. Emma not only led several to Christ, but she also helped heal generations of brokenness and pain.

Emma is now married to an incredible man who loves her deeply. Their marriage is a model for healthy love and attachment. She is walking in the redemption and healing only the Lord can provide. And she's a mom to three beautiful children whom she chooses to bless and affirm each and every day.

Emma, through God's blessing, has truly reversed the curse. And while the pictures of her painful past are still there, they have been rewritten by the Lord, have been covered in His healing, and are now used to display His light and love to others who are struggling.

If you think you may have missed the Blessing from a parent or other significant person in your life, we hope to walk you through the same process of reversing the curse that Emma went through. It began with the choice you made at the start of this chapter.

Next we'll help you understand whether in fact you received the Blessing. To do this, we'll look at the five elements of the Blessing and uncover their presence or absence in your life story. Then we'll look at five types of homes that withhold the Blessing and the common results of growing up in such cultures of subtraction.

We'll also dig deeper into the pictures of your life story and walk through the healing process of allowing the Lord to access and redeem the moments that need His love, light, and blessing.

Then we'll get immensely practical as we discover seven powerful tools for change, and we'll end with a twenty-eight-day plan to help you put everything you've learned into action. So let's get started. We begin by discovering why it hurts so much if we didn't get the Blessing.

PART ONE

IT BEGINS WITH WHAT WE MISSED

*It is all backwards when a torn pattern—a spoiled pattern—
is followed and handed down year after year, and people
forget what the original pattern was like. It is all backwards
when men turn from God because they can't stand the
word* father *and thus attribute wrong things to God.*

EDITH SCHAEFFER, *A Way of Seeing*

CHAPTER 3

WHY IT HURTS SO MUCH TO MISS THE BLESSING

Think back to when you were ten years old. Imagine that you're walking up to your house. It's early evening, growing dark, and it looks as if every light has been turned on inside your house.

As you get to the window and lean forward to look inside, you can see there's a party going on, or at least some kind of gathering. (And yes, if your home growing up was a sixth-floor condo or second-story apartment, you're able to levitate and look in the window and see everyone. Remember, we're imagining here.)

There, all together inside the same room and busy talking with each other, is *every significant person in your ten-year-old life story.* For example, I (John) would see my mother, my grandmother, and my mother's sister, Aunt Dovie, who lived with us. And of course I'd see my two brothers. There would also be Senator Sam Smorgasbord Sad Apple Trent, our huge, brown-and-white English bulldog whose extra-large personality required several names. And let's not forget the imperious Siamese who let us all live there, Mr. Cat (so named because my brothers and I were very creative).

That would have been all the key players who were a constant in my life at ten years old. Now it's your turn. Who would be inside that room for you?

With your nose right up to the window, in your mind's eye, one by one, each person will turn and look at you.

It's that immediate, unscripted reaction when they see you unexpectedly that we want you to imagine.

One at a time, as they look up and see you, what would that first glance reveal? How would it register in your mind's eye and heart?

Would that person's eyes fly wide open and light up with delight? Would there be an immediate smile that followed? Would the person point at you or even call out your name, excited to see you? Would he or she take a step toward you to welcome you in? And even though you can't hear the words from outside, can you see the person mouthing something like "Yay! It's you!" or "Look who's here!" with genuine joy?

Or—and please be honest—as each person takes a turn looking at you, is there one or more who rolls his eyes when he sees you? Does one give you an angry stare or a dismissive look? Does anyone quickly look away, hoping you didn't notice her catching sight of you? Or was there a look like someone was simply tired of dealing with you, as if you had to be put up with, not welcomed?

Even worse, did anyone have a "still-face" look?

We're referring to a well-known experiment with the same name in which a video begins showing a mother and her young daughter, not even two years old.[1] At first, the mother responds to her child's every noise and action. She's the model of a loving, caring parent. Her daughter loves her back in her own way for being present, alert, smiling, and tender with her. You get the impression that all this positive parenting is the normal way this mother and child interact.

But after this time of positive interaction, the mother turns her head away.

There is a long pause.

Then she turns back toward her child and goes "still face."

Picture *zero emotional reaction on her face.* Besides blinking or breathing, she makes literally zero emotional response. Even her eyes seem dead. She says nothing no matter what happens. There's no shaking of the head or hint of a smile in the eyes.

Go find a mirror and try doing that. It's not easy when you're just looking at yourself. It's even more difficult with a real person in front of you. And it takes a herculean effort not to give away even a hint of a smile or frown when a small child is valiantly trying to get some kind of reaction from you.

Yet you're watching that mother show zero emotion. *Flat affect.* And immediately the child realizes that something significant has changed. Even at that young age, in her heart, she knows something has gone terribly wrong.

She's confused. But she can't talk yet, so she starts to make noises. Then she tries pointing (like she did earlier, which had received a positive reaction from her mother). This time, there is no response to her pointing. No movement. No acknowledgment.

If you've seen this video, the next few minutes are heartbreaking. The longer the mother just sits there still face, the more the child reacts. She starts to screech. *That doesn't work.* She looks sad. *That doesn't work.* She even begins to throw herself from side to side.

She is doing anything she can to try to get her mother to see her. To come back to her. To be with her. To respond to her.

Finally, the mother does stop the still-face act and goes back to being warmly interactive. But in an eerie way, you're left with a sense that, experiment or not, just those two minutes of still face will leave a mark.

Now, what if that was the look you got almost every day?

For some of us, that was our reality. And just like that precious little girl in the still-face experiment, we tried everything we could think of to get that person's attention and affirmation—from good behavior to bad. Each failed attempt dug us deeper and deeper into despair. Many of us finally just gave up, believing that somehow, at our core, we were undeserving, unworthy, or not important or talented enough to receive the love and acceptance—or even comfort—we needed.

This lack of relational engagement is profound. And it can shape not only how we view ourselves, but also how we view every significant relationship in our lives. After all, if we believe in our heart of hearts that we're unlovable, a whole host of relational issues can arise—from staying in unhealthy and damaging relationships to living with insecurity and abandonment issues and everything in between.

We're praying that you had someone in that imaginary room, at that crucial ten-year-old time in your life, whose eyes opened wide and lit up when he saw you. That you had even *one person* whose initial reaction was joy, who lovingly moved toward you.

If we believe in our heart of hearts that we're unlovable, a whole host of relational issues can arise.

And yes, we're talking about people, but we put the pets in the room on purpose. It's amazing how many people we work and talk with who can't think of a *single person* who would have welcomed them or responded warmly at that age. But when pressed, their eyes will often look up and to the left (accessing the part of the brain that goes to our mental pictures). It's like watching them search through a mental photo album. And suddenly they'll remember someone—that beloved pet who was crazy about them. (Which is why, in part, we think the Lord gave us dogs.)

In my home at ten, Mr. Cat would not have reacted to me *or anyone* in any way other than dismissively. But if Senator Sam the bulldog saw any one of us three boys, you were about to see an explosion of fur. Whether we'd been gone from his presence for five hours or five minutes, the same thing always happened.

We're not talking about the wonderful small French bulldogs so popular today. We're talking a living Mack Trucks emblem. A very large, very heavy, slobbering, snorting English bulldog.

When Sam saw you, it would begin with a full-body, uncontrollable moment of in-place shimmying, wagging, and whimpering. Then that ball of love and affection would hurl himself at you, as if he were being launched off an aircraft carrier. Sam would plow through anything or anyone on his way to ramming into your legs and demanding to be hugged and petted, saying without words that you'd been gone far too long and how much he'd missed you.

It made you feel wonderful.

To be lovingly attacked by Sam was a gift. Even after the most difficult day at school, nothing could stand up to that kind of unbridled affection.

Thankfully, along with Sam, there were others in my home who were also excited to see me when I was ten. They, too, would look up in love and welcome me—without the slobbering.

We hope that was your story. That there was someone there for you. Lord willing, more than one someone. But we do live in a real world. And since you've picked up this book, there's a good chance your past may have been more like Steve Martin's.

The Greatest Comedian with the Greatest Childhood Ever

The poignant, revealing documentary *Steve! (Martin): A Documentary in 2 Pieces*[2] shows how one of the world's most successful stand-up comics began his career.

Steve Martin was ten years old in 1955. He was growing up in beautiful Southern California. His home was in Garden Grove, right next to Anaheim. And in Anaheim, Disneyland had opened! Then Steve heard that Disneyland was hiring ten-year-olds to sell the daily Disneyland park newspaper to people walking into the park.

It meant he could work for a few hours in the morning but then he'd be free to roam anywhere around the happiest place on earth! He could go on rides over and over. He could wander into any of the attractions he wanted as many times as he wanted. It made a huge impact on Martin's life. He recalls, "I remember thinking I had this happy, happiest childhood—happiest, it was so happy— and then later I realized that *Oh yeah, happy outside the house.*"

Did your heart just sink when you read that last sentence?

Perhaps because you can relate?

If you were going to find any fun or magic, attachment or warmth, it meant going somewhere else. A neighbor's home. Your grandparents' home. Even to school. But never at your home.

Did you wonder why we had you pick ten years old to imagine looking inside your home? It's because age ten is when most children begin moving from concrete to abstract reasoning. Before then, children will likely believe every home and all families on their street experience life much as they do. But around age ten, boys and girls begin to realize that's not true.

At Disneyland, Steve Martin found fun, laughter, connection, joy, affirmation, and friendship. He got to know the comedian at the Golden Horseshoe Revue. He ended up watching that comedy show hundreds of times over the years. Then his big break came when his dream job opened up. It was a sales position in a Disneyland magic shop. At that time, it was in a beautiful cottage next to the endlessly photographed Sleeping Beauty Castle.

All day, day after day, along with his magic skills, Martin was building his people and comedic skills. He was meeting hundreds of people from everywhere, doing tricks and shaping balloon animals for them. In the process, he'd try to sell them something. And for fun and as a way of quickly connecting with people, he'd crack jokes that he and his best friend and coworker would make up or borrow from other comedians. If the joke worked, they'd use it on the next person. If it failed, they'd improvise or improve it or finally toss it—all this with a friend and coworker who shared Martin's love of surprising and entertaining people.

Think about all those positives again. Connection, caring, laughter, friendship, fellowship. Not to mention all that positive vision casting of who he could become. All captured inside the "happiest place on earth."

And then he'd go home.

Watching the documentary, you begin to realize from the still pictures displayed, the home movies of Martin and his family, and the commentary in the film that there was no magic in his home. What waited for him was either still face or angry face.

There was no spontaneous joy when he walked in, particularly in his interactions with his father. Perhaps you know what that feels like.

"So the Blessing is all about that one look someone chooses to give or not give you when you come home?"

Actually, neurologically, that one look *is* incredibly important and can say a tremendous amount about who truly cared for you and who didn't. We're wired to see and search for threats and for people who provide a sense of safety—in many ways, to see who in our lives is blessing us and who isn't.

You see a powerful example of the importance of this look in Scripture. Psalm 16:11 is a beautiful verse that many people memorize. Many others buy it stitched on a pillow or painted on a plaque to display in their home. The verse reads, in part, "In Your presence is fullness of joy."

Guess what "in Your presence" literally means in Hebrew, the language of the Old Testament? It means, "When I see Your face."

In God's face you see joy. It's not some kind of plastic, two-dimensional smiley face. In the face of the Lord of lords and King of kings, you find fullness of joy. He's someone whose face actually does light up when He sees you, bringing delight and joy with that look.

In another verse we read, "The eyes of the LORD roam throughout the earth, so that He may strongly support those whose heart is completely His" (2 Chronicles 16:9). You may have the picture of a God whose only look is an angry one because that's the look you received most often at home. But His eyes are searching out ways to support and lift you up. That's the kind of eyes you want on you!

We see something similar said of Jesus' face as well: "For God, who said, 'Light shall shine out of darkness,' is the One who has shone in our hearts to give the Light of the knowledge of the glory of God *in the face of Christ*" (2 Corinthians 4:6, emphasis added).

What Does Joy Have to Do with the Blessing?

In the outstanding book *The Other Half of Church*, written by our friends Jim Wilder and Michel Hendricks, Jim recounts his work with noted UCLA brain researcher Dr. Allan Schore. Dr. Schore focused his study on how the human brain develops through *joy* and *attachment*. Dr. Schore would emphasize in all his talks the importance of joy in healthy brain development. He defined someone who displays joy relationally as "someone who is glad to be with me" and *"being the sparkle in someone's eye."*[3]

Even if we try to deny or ignore it, if there was no joy in your childhood home, almost certainly there was no blessing.

Kari and I will often ask people we're working with, "Who was it who, when they looked at you, you just knew they were crazy about you?" Like when you were ten years old and looking through a window. We'll talk more about brain research and the Blessing in a later chapter. But know that there is often a difficult reality: If there was no one whose face reflected joy and love when he looked at you, even occasionally, his actions in most cases would not be to bless. Even if you try to deny or ignore it, if there was no joy in your childhood home, almost certainly there was no blessing. Not that someone's face had to break out in a smile or bright eyes *every* time she saw you. *Everyone has bad days or weeks.*

Giving the Blessing doesn't have to be done perfectly, but it does need to be *consistent.* At least some of the time, you should have received that positive look. But if there was little or no joy ever, likely there would be little love or blessing in your home.

How people looked at you growing up does matter. So does receiving or missing the five elements of the Blessing, as you'll see. If they're not present, it leaves a mark deep inside.

You might argue, "Of course I got the Blessing! After all, that person paid for the new car that I got to show off in high school" or "He covered my college tuition." Such a person may have been generous or even extravagant, but you can't buy joy or the Blessing.

The Blessing is relational, not transactional.

That's why it hurts so much when we never received it, when we never saw it in the face of a loved one nor ever received the five elements that were always part of giving the Blessing in Scripture.

Wherever He entered villages, or cities, or a countryside,
they were laying the sick in the marketplaces and
imploring Him that they might just touch the fringe
of His cloak; and all who touched it were being healed.

MARK 6:56

I remember another picture. A picture of Dad rubbing
my legs when he tucked me in bed. "Growing pains,"
he called them. I remember those pains waking me up
in the middle of the night. And however late, however
often, he would come and rub the hurt away.

KEN GIRE, *The Gift of Remembrance*

CHAPTER 4

WHEN WE MISS THE FIRST ELEMENT: APPROPRIATE, MEANINGFUL TOUCH

To help you further evaluate whether you received the Blessing, let's look closer at the five elements of the biblical blessing we've mentioned. Here they are:

Appropriate, Meaningful Touch
Spoken Words
Attaching High Value
Picturing a Special Future
Genuine Commitment

If a red flag (or even a yellow one) goes up in your mind at the mere mention of the word *touch*, please note the words *appropriate* and *meaningful* that preface it. We understand that touch is broken in many ways today. Many have added a default setting to their lives that says that any touch is more of a curse than any kind of blessing. That's a common reaction to being hurt physically. But cutting off all appropriate touch isn't physically or emotionally healthy at any time in your life.

In Scripture, we see an act of touch being part of the Blessing time and again. The Holy Spirit comes down to land on Jesus' shoulder. We see a hug being given from a father to a son. And there's the laying on of hands by a grandfather with his grandsons. We see two warriors (David and Jonathan) embrace. And of course we see Jesus doing things like reaching out and touching and blessing an "untouchable" leper when He heals him. Other times, He would heal without any act of touch, but with this leper, who was denied physical contact with anyone, He reversed the curse and touched him. And of course we see Jesus rebuking the disciples who had shooed away the children; instead "He took them in His arms and began blessing them, laying His hands on them" (Mark 10:16).

But why is touch so significant, and why is it so hurtful if we miss it?

If you think about newborns: What's the first sense they have? It's not their precious eyesight, which can't focus yet to clearly see you. They're easily startled by noises because their sense of sound isn't well developed. Of our five senses, the one that comes wide awake first for babies is their tactile sense.

They sense whether the world around them is warm or cold. They reach out instinctively for someone, even right after birth. Their little fingers and hands search for someone who will reach back. They nod toward a nipple to be fed and love being comforted by being wrapped up tight and held close.

As we grow up, it is the *tenderness* of touch that continues to communicate a lot. If we were only touched in anger or pushed aside in indifference, however, we have missed out on a deep need we all have.

Picture a child in a thunderstorm running into a parent's arms. He needs to know with that touch, even more than with words right then, that he's not alone. That things will be all right. That someone is there to help.

Touch can do all that without a word being spoken.

Did You Have to Kiss Yourself Goodnight?

Appropriate, meaningful touch is what a two-year-old who has fallen asleep experiences when she's lovingly carried off to bed. It's what we experience when we're hurting and alone and He holds us tight. It's what touch can do for all of us. For touch, in its best form, bonds us with others, particularly when our need is great, lifting our spirits and calming our hearts.

But for too many of us, it simply wasn't there. Consider the woman who told us, "When bedtime came as a child, I would hug myself to sleep. I would kiss my arm goodnight."

If that was your story, then to see what the lack of touch can do, just turn its many benefits around. If attachment means that someone is reaching back when you reach out, missing this element of the Blessing means that no one reached back.

If no one's arms are there to hug away the hurt, there is that deep memory of being left in fear or the conclusion that no one was ever coming and you would have to face things alone.

There's a therapeutic term for what happens when attachment is broken. When appropriate, meaningful touch is cut off. When no one reaches back.

Primal panic.

This is much different from just being alone. Many of us live alone. Missing the Blessing isn't about being single or living alone where there isn't someone else physically present to touch us regularly. That's very different from never remembering been held, soothed, or touched in a loving, appropriate way as a child.

Let's go back to that sudden thunderstorm that scared a child into a loved one's arms. As you think back on your life, can you remember when touch went missing? For many of us, it wasn't just one thunderstorm where we weren't soothed with a tender touch. There were countless opportunities when someone important to us *could* have reached back. Could have given us a hug. Even just shaken our hand or laid a hand on our shoulder. But all those times, that someone chose not to say with touch that he or she loved us.

If no one reached back when you reached out, you've definitely missed the first element of the Blessing.

We know that for many of you, touch may have been used as a curse—not just withheld. Abuse of any kind is the opposite of blessing. And please know that if this is your story, you're not alone. There is help and hope available, even if you've never addressed that part of your story before.

If no one reached back when you reached out, you've definitely missed the first element of the Blessing.

I (Kari) was blessed to grow up with tons of appropriate, meaningful touch in my home. However, after I left my abusive relationship with my ex-husband, touch had a totally different meaning. It was no longer safe, comforting, and protective. Instead, it felt dangerous, threatening, and harmful. However, over time, with God's help and the help of a fantastic counselor, this element of the Blessing has been restored and is something I now actively enjoy with my husband and our family. I hope my young boys know that it's always available for them.

Nothing is too big for God. Even if reaching out to others or experiencing healing and restorative touch seems impossible today, that does not have to define your life or relationships moving forward.

[Saying "I love you" is] the oxygen for the relationship. . . . Telling somebody you love them feeds the relationship, keeps it alive.

DR. LISA ARANGO,
quoted in "Why You Should Say 'I Love You' Today—and Always"

CHAPTER 5

WHEN WE MISS THE SECOND ELEMENT: SPOKEN WORDS

Life can be challenging. Maybe you're facing skyrocketing inflation that makes you wonder if you'll ever be able to keep up. Perhaps wars are breaking out worldwide or, closer to home, riots and road blockages seem to be popping up everywhere. Maybe you're part of the vast group of men and women who self-report that they can't name even a single good friend.

Sound anything like your life today?

Yet there's something that can be a tremendous help to a troubled heart. It's the second element of the Blessing that we hope you received growing up: *spoken words.*

Imagine you're right there with what we shared above. You're living in tough times. You're having a difficult time holding your head up, and you're struggling and discouraged. On top of that, you're feeling lonely and unwanted. You're convinced that you're *not* as strong or as smart as everyone around you—certainly not as courageous.

But then it happens. The second element of the Blessing shows up.

And when it does, your outlook on life and who you are changes. Why? Someone significant in your life has sat down next to you, someone you regard as wise, brave, and smart. And that someone takes your hand, looks you right in the eyes, and says,

You're braver than you believe,
and stronger than you seem,
and smarter than you think.
But the most important thing is,
even if we are apart,
I'll always be with you.

Do you know who needs those encouraging words? If your first thought was *I do!*, we're with you. *Join the club!*

Actually, those words were spoken to a sad, frightened, discouraged, and downcast *bear* named Winnie the Pooh.

And the person who said them? He was the person Pooh loved most in all the world and who loved him back. *Christopher Robin.*

You'll find the scene in the animated movie *Pooh's Grand Adventure: The Search for Christopher Robin.*[1] Short clips are available online, and some have gathered well over 4.5 million views to date. I'm sure many people have watched them once and then hit replay to watch them again. *Some have watched that scene many times over* because just *hearing spoken words* can be healing, be it in animation or in real life.

Positive spoken words can encourage us. They can help us deal with what's wrong on the outside and with doubts we have on the inside. They can bring rest to our hearts.

Spoken words also require someone to take action, as God the Father did in giving us His Word, Jesus. God didn't just *think about* sending His Son. "In the beginning was the Word, and the Word was with God, and the Word was God. . . . And the Word became flesh, and dwelt among us" (John 1:1, 14).

We need spoken words of blessing. We need to hear that God

chooses us, cares for us, and will never bail on us. But we also need to hear these spoken words from a parent or other loved one.

Real life isn't always as encouraging as it was for Pooh in the Hundred Acre Wood, however. We may not have had a wise, loving Christopher Robin to provide the spoken words that can mean a lot to us. If we missed the Blessing, we're more likely to have heard words like these:

- "How can you think a fat mess like you would ever get a date?"
- "Don't talk about taking calculus! That's for the smart kids!"
- "You? Trying out for choir? I've heard frogs croak better than you sing."

Or the words one new mother told us that were her undoing:

"A girl? You had a girl? I should have known you'd have a girl."

There are countless discouraging, disheartening spoken words that can be whispered or shouted at us if we missed the Blessing. Words that push us down. Attack our person, character, or physical attributes. Words that try to dash any hope we have of doing better, downplaying the very outcome of our lives.

You may say, "My parents spoke cruel words and discouraging things to me all the time, but it just made me want to prove them wrong! I went out and did what they said I couldn't!"

For every child who hears negative words and then decides to shout back, "You're wrong!" and goes on to charge up the hill to victory, there are five hundred more who will withdraw rather than fight.

After all, the negative words are being spoken by, of all people, *their parents*. A father who has seen them since their birth. A mother who knows them better than anyone else in all the world. The authority figure in their early lives who should affirm them but verbally tears them down instead.

As we'll see shortly when we look at certain homes that with-hold the Blessing, even for those who do set out to prove their parents wrong, success can fail to really set things right. We recall the person we worked with who spent every day focused on exceeding his parents' net worth, which was significant. And he finally did! Yet on that day, looking at his Fidelity balance sheet didn't bring the elation he sought. He just felt more emptiness! That was the day he knew he needed counseling.

It's a hollow victory when we try to earn the gift of our parents' blessing.

It's a hollow victory when we try to *earn* the gift of our parents' blessing. Because if we're honest, all our efforts still have never been affirmed! We're still in search of the words of blessing.

And one more thing before we go on to the next element: We bless someone when we say affirming words. *We choose to emotionally damage someone when we say nothing at all.*

Unspoken Words Can Create Orphans at Home

Over the years, we've worked with many people who didn't hear negative words at home. They heard something that's often worse—near silence when it came to spoken words about them. Growing up in an environment where few words of encouragement or affirmation were shared, they felt ignored, unwanted, like orphans at home.

One person asked us, "Do you know what song is at the top of my playlist?" It wasn't a song like "A Beautiful Morning" or "Celebration." Instead it was "The Greatest Man I Never Knew."

If you're not familiar with this song, it's sung by a daughter about her father, who has just passed away. He was the greatest man she never knew. "The one who lived just down the hall . . . but never made any attempt to bridge the gap of silence."[2]

Many of us who tried to engage with a non-engaging parent can relate. I (John) can remember desperately wanting to talk with my father. And, amazingly, the opportunity did come one day toward the end of his life. He had gone through heart surgery, and he had nowhere to convalesce for several weeks. So I talked with my wife, Cindy, and we invited him into our home.

I was in my forties then. For the first time in my memory, I spent the night under the same roof as my father. I relished the thought. I had been trained to ask questions as a counselor. I'm good at it. Like many people who have that outgoing "Otter" per-sonality,[3] I'm good at getting people to open up. I can draw things out of people, even those who are hesitant or initially unwilling.

Well, for more than a month, I tried everything. But my father was like that man in the song. That's why the first time I actually heard "The Greatest Man I Never Knew," I had to pull my car off the road because I was crying so hard.

After so many years and so much absence, I just knew that God was giving me an opportunity to break through. To get my father to finally open up his heart and life. To fill in many blanks. To get on the kind of topics that would mean a lot not just to me but also to my brothers and my own children.

In all the days under the same roof, however, I got nothing from him. Sometimes he'd smile quickly. He'd say a few words after I'd ask a question. Then he'd deflect or step away. He wouldn't bite when I offered words or questions about his life growing up. He wouldn't go into any detail on any of his life experiences—not just about the war he fought in, but even about things I thought would be easy to talk about, like his work, his living with my uncle, Max, or his life on the farm with his brothers.

He was there for a month, and he remained the greatest man I never knew.

Unspoken words of blessing or people who block any attempts

at connection can leave just as big a hole in our hearts as hearing discouraging words. Their absence can leave us feeling incomplete, like there's a missing sense of who we are. And we don't know how to fill in the blank, or if we ever can.

Without Spoken Words, Our Cravings Increase

Finally, without spoken words, we often become starved for praise or affirmation. We're especially eager for positive spoken words that *might* have been said about us!

Can you see how this craving can be magnified on social media? *Did I get enough likes? Why did someone else get more likes than I did when what I said was so much cooler (or more significant)? Why are* they *being lifted up or talked about and not me?*

Missing out on spoken words can supercharge our need for affirmation and attachment. And in the process it blocks us from doing something emotionally healthy people can do: "Rejoice with those who rejoice, and weep with those who weep" (Romans 12:15).

When we miss hearing spoken words of blessing, we can become so focused on what's missing that we struggle to celebrate or to grieve with anyone else. After all, that person may be hurting, but *what about us?* What about our needs and hurts? What about all those times we weren't comforted? Yes, that person is celebrating, *but shouldn't I be getting some of that attention?* In short, *life without spoken words of blessing is often life lived only about us.*

Life without spoken words of blessing is often life lived only about us.

We can become so self-absorbed with feeling unimportant or unvalued that we're not free to serve, bless, comfort, or celebrate with others. We haven't heard the spoken words that can bring rest to our souls and hearts. And neither do we believe that we have high value in who we are now or who we can become—which is the next element of the Blessing.

I had not noticed how the humblest, and at the same time most balanced and capacious, minds praised most, while the cranks, misfits, and malcontents praised least. The good critics found something to praise in many imperfect works; the bad ones continually narrowed the list of books we might be allowed to read.

C. S. LEWIS, *Reflections on the Psalms*

CHAPTER 6

WHEN WE MISS
THE THIRD ELEMENT:
ATTACHING HIGH VALUE

Let's look one more time at the documentary on Steve Martin's life, this time later in Martin's life, where the filmmakers focus on a story that's also in his autobiography, which is titled *Born Standing Up*.

Martin had just finished the most successful tour of any stand-up comic ever. He had just spent sixty days doing fifty sold-out, standing-room-only stadium and concert-hall events across the country. In doing so, he had crushed records and received rave reviews.

Then, with the tour over, after he had done more than any other stand-up comedian, Steve Martin decided, *That's it*. Not *it* as in he was going to quit everything or retire but *it* as in he was making a career move.

He would stop doing stand-up comedy. He would move on to starring on the big screen.

In most cases, even for highly successful people, that's a mistake of epic proportions. Historically, stars who switch from one major area of success to another usually fail miserably.

For example, how often do you sit around on a Saturday night with your friends and hear someone say, "Hey, I know! Let's watch an Elvis movie or two!"

Has that ever happened?

Sadly, those Elvis movies were more fads than great cinematic attractions. The more movies Elvis did, the more his fans wished he would (and were glad when he did) finally go back to singing.

It's hard to switch platforms, much less hit gold twice.

Yet that didn't stop Steve Martin. He went from crushing stand-up comedy to helping write and then star in his breakout movie, *The Jerk*. And—in case you didn't see it—it *wasn't* a flop. It was poorly reviewed by some critics (because it was, admittedly, bizarre), but normal moviegoing people *loved* it. It grossed more than $70 million at the US box office alone! That amount in 1979 would equate to $317,167,208 today![1]

Though we can't endorse all of them because of content issues, Martin would go on to star in several more incredibly successful movies, like *Planes, Trains and Automobiles*, and a hugely popular television series, *Only Murders in the Building*. But let's go back to that first movie and what happened there. It says a lot about our need to have someone important give us the third element of the Blessing: *attaching high value.*

On the night *The Jerk* premiered in Hollywood, Martin asked his father to come with him to the theater and go with him and several friends to a private dinner afterward.

Martin's father agreed, and they all watched the movie in the sold-out theater and then went to dinner. But at dinner, after a long period of unrelated, inconsequential conversations, one of Martin's friends finally asked the question that seemed to be the elephant in the room.

"Glenn," he said to Steve's father, "what did you think of Steve's movie?"[2]

His response was "Well . . ." Long pause. "He's no Charlie Chaplin."

That was it.

No spoken positive words. Just caustic sarcasm from an unkind heart. No words that attached high value; just words that almost certainly came from a person who had never heard affirming words himself.

That's often what has happened when we've missed the Blessing. If we step back and look at our own parents' lives, we'll see that *they missed the Blessing.* Maybe they missed out on people seeing and pointing to any high value they had. Often, their own parents were blind to anything positive they might have done as children.

Consider George Brett, one of Major League Baseball's most famous players. He came the closest to tying or breaking Ted Williams's record of hitting .406 for the season (a record that still stands today).

In 1980, it looked like Brett would do it! But when the season ended, his batting average sat at .390. It was a *huge* achievement in Major League Baseball, one of the best batting averages ever, and Brett would go on to become a first-ballot Hall of Famer.

But what did he hear from his father?

"You couldn't have gotten five more hits?"[3]

George Brett had nearly broken Ted Williams's record, yet he heard no words that attached high value. Steve Martin had just hit it out of the park in ways that no one had done before in both stand-up comedy *and* a major motion picture. Yet he heard nothing but words that dismissed what he'd done.

How do efforts like Brett's and Martin's not rate some words of praise or affirmation? What is it that keeps a parent from giving this third element of the Blessing?

The whole world could see what amazing things these two had done. But there was no recognition of their achievements from those closest to them. No "I'm so proud of you, Son." No "This is my beloved son!"

Can you relate to not hearing words that attached high value to you at a key time in your life? Or ever? Again, achievement doesn't earn us the Blessing. But expressing a child's high value is a response that comes naturally from a loving heart.

What blocks someone from seeing what others see clearly, things that God sees in our lives?

When It Seems as if a Parent Has on Blinders

If you never heard words that attached high value to who you were as a person, in most cases it was as if your parents had on blinders. If they never commented on things you worked hard to accomplish—even if you did fall short by five hits—then they purposely put them on. But in most cases, they were blind to seeing value in you because they saw no high value in themselves.

Almost always, people who can't attach high value to others have missed the Blessing themselves.

Almost always, people who can't attach high value to others have missed the Blessing themselves. They can't shine a spotlight on anyone else because that would be a reminder that they never had it pointed at them.

Was that true in your life story? Did someone put on blinders and withhold words that attached high value to you? If so, that can affect how you look at yourself now and, tragically, in the future as well.

That brings us to the next element of the Blessing.

We—or at least I—shall not be able to adore God on the highest occasions if we have learned no habit of doing so on the lowest. . . . Any patch of sunlight in a wood will show you something about the sun which you could never get from reading books on astronomy. These pure and spontaneous pleasures are "patches of Godlight" in the woods of our experience.

C. S. LEWIS, *Letters to Malcolm: Chiefly on Prayer*

CHAPTER 7

WHEN WE MISS THE FOURTH ELEMENT: PICTURING A SPECIAL FUTURE

Here's another question we often ask those struggling with having missed the Blessing: *As you were growing up, who said something that made you think,* I can head that direction! *or* Maybe I could be good at that? That's the fourth part of the Blessing: *picturing a special future.*

We're not talking here about what you hear at nearly every three- or four-year-old's soccer practice, where every halfway-successful team effort is applauded. With the Blessing, picturing a special future is *personal*. It's what someone significant in your life sees about *your* story and *the direction your life might take.*

This takes us to another question: *Was there someone in your life who seemed to be able to see, even if you couldn't back then, the early dawn of the kind of future you could have?*

Granted, some of us have a sibling who just seemed to know from his earliest years what he was going to do. My twin brother, Jeff, for example, knew at age five or six that he was going to be a doctor and started planning for it. He talked our mother into buying him two baseball gloves. That way he could play half the game right-handed and half the game left-handed. And he would start the school day writing left-handed and then switch to writing right-handed after lunch. Why? He knew that if he went into surgery, he'd need to be able to use either hand. What a shock: He did, in fact, become a board-certified cancer doctor and world-renowned personalized medicine geneticist!

For most of us, however, what *might* happen in our future seemed far murkier when we were young. I'm reminded of something that happened when I was the commencement speaker at Azusa Pacific University.

I had given my speech, and the students had paraded across the stage to receive their diplomas. When the students were all back in their seats, just before they were formally announced by the school president to have graduated, they were each given a large balloon.

The announcement came that they had graduated, and everyone was told to let go of his or her balloon. Graduation caps went up in the air, and so did all the balloons. But as I watched, something interesting happened.

I'm sure whoever had supplied the balloons had worked long and hard filling several hundred of them with helium. Nonetheless, a number of the students' balloons didn't immediately go up. Many did, racing high into the sky. But a great many others took their time lifting off. Some seemed to mill around, slowly gaining altitude. Then all of a sudden they picked up speed like they were chasing the others heading out of sight. Still others floated sideways. A few barely got off the ground at all.

That's a good picture of how many of us figure out what we're to do in life! What we're really good at. What we can become. What we can do and where we should go.

That's also why many of us benefit greatly when someone else sees our strengths or gifts or special future and tells us about it!

"I Don't Care What That Teacher Says."

When I (John) began to study this element of the Blessing, both in Scripture and in clinical literature on attachment and relationships, few studies used the actual word *attachment*. Today, however, *attachment* is *the* key word of choice for building loving bonds in children's and adults' relationships. And an often-cited way to build attachment is to picture a special future for someone. The idea is that recognizing and pointing out a person's gifts or God-given abilities can make a difference in his or her life. At the least, it can give a person that nudge toward figuring out his or her calling.

For me, a major barrier to thinking I had any kind of future besides asking people "Paper or plastic?" was The Mother of All Term Papers at the very end of high school. This paper stood between me and graduating or taking another year to do so. And it hung like a wet, heavy albatross around my neck.

My problem wasn't being compared to my all-everything twin brother. It was that I didn't think school mattered! That showed up in poor grades and came down to my senior-year English class and end-of-year massive term paper.

I went to school at a time when the system still failed students if their grades weren't high enough or they didn't complete an important class. So it had all come down to that term paper on the Battle of the Bulge. I had picked that decisive World War II battle as my topic. And it had become a fierce fight to see whether I was going to graduate.

I worked hard (for me) on the paper. But while Jeff had started two months ahead of time on his paper, I'd started a near-record (for me) two *days* ahead of time to create my masterpiece of military history. I even stayed up almost all night before it was due typing my paper.

That's when I ran out of typewriter ribbon. For people today, that wouldn't be an issue. You'd just go to the all-night Walmart and get another ink cartridge for your printer. Or, more realistically, you'd be submitting it to your school's online portal and wouldn't have to print it at all.

But back then, there were no Walmarts in Arizona—no stores of any kind that were open at two o'clock in the morning selling typewriter ribbons. And no internet. So I handwrote the last few pages.

But despite some obvious *minor* flaws, like skipping footnotes (which looked hard) and the handwriting issue, I was convinced I'd pass with more than flying colors. I had convinced myself that after years of hearing "Why can't you be like your brother?" this time I was going to hear "Wow! Your paper is so much better than your brother's!"

In the movie *A Christmas Story*, Ralphie has to write a theme. On the day his paper is handed back, in his mind's eye, he's carried around the class by cheering students with his teacher at the chalkboard writing "A++" in big script.

On the day I received back my term paper, let's just say "A+" wasn't on the last page. After all the other red marks on every page was a huge D–. Not a B–, which would have been way better than most of my papers, but that scarlet letter *D* and the minus sign that you could tell she had added with a flourish.

While I celebrated and joked about it with my friends, inside it made me feel like an idiot and a failure.

And then came the words she'd written underneath: *"I gave you a D because I don't want to see you next year."*

That did two things. First, it said I would graduate—not with honors like my brother, but at least I could walk with everyone else, which would make my grandmother very happy. And second, while I celebrated and joked about it with my friends, inside it made me feel like an idiot and a failure.

Here, then, is where the fourth element of the Blessing comes in. That night, my precious mother sat me down at our kitchen table. She was persistent in wanting to see the paper she knew I'd worked hard on. I finally dug it out of my bag and handed it over.

She read it all. Finally, after the last page of red marks and critical commentary, she came to the end. She stopped, and you could tell she was reading and rereading what the teacher had written.

At last she spoke. What followed weren't words of how this was proof I shouldn't pursue anything in life that involved academics or writing. She saw something else. She saw a special future in that mess of a paper that was the capstone of four years of underachieving in high school.

"Look at me," my mother said.

As I'd been sitting there, my head had been dropping lower and lower with each page she had read.

"Look at me, John," she said, and I finally looked up into those beautiful, unique, gunmetal-blue eyes.

"I don't care what that teacher says. You do such a good job of using words. I wouldn't be surprised if God used your words someday to help others."

I could see that she meant it, and something came alive in my heart. I had worked hard. I thought that parts of the paper really were well written. But hearing her words brought a light for a path that my teachers didn't see then (and rightly so). It was a light I needed desperately, a picture (to change the metaphor) of a special future that *might* be true. Perhaps *could* come true. Those words helped me see that maybe I could do something valuable in the future. Perhaps I could do something with writing to help others.

Take Your Pick of Reasons Why Today There Is No Future

Time and again when the Blessing is given in Scripture, it is linked with a person's future, not just his or her life at the moment. A blessing is something a child or loved one carries that holds out hope for tomorrow.

We're aware that in every generation past, there have been huge challenges. Worldwide pandemics, world wars. Things that have led people to wonder if the future would be positive or terrible. But there's a huge difference today.

Instead of just a few street-corner fatalists with signs saying "The world is ending!" that message is *exactly* what's being taught in high schools and colleges as so-called settled science. A small number of anarchists and fatalists, with a major media microphone and control over school curricula, are telling even young children that there is no special future for anyone. There is no habitable, positive, beautiful, challenging world in their tomorrow.

And with that being taught and chanted, many younger people are saying, "If that's true, why bother to make a plan? If there's no future, why get married? Why start a family and bring an innocent child into all this? Why invest in anything that takes time to go up in value (like a house I can't afford anyway)? I'll just rent and spend whatever I have now. No reason to save toward something that'll all come apart anyway."

Perhaps even worse: "If there's no future, don't waste time on love and joy and hope. All that's left is for us to be angry! To choose death over life, curse over blessing. To tear things down."

But along comes God's loving, encouraging, life-changing Word. And it lays out a totally different future—a totally different choice we must confront in this world trying to erase our choices.

In Deuteronomy 30:19, we read, "I have placed before you life and death, the blessing and the curse. So choose life in order that you may live, you and your descendants."

God both sets before us a choice and gives us the correct answer to the test: Choose life and blessing. It's the opposite of what the world is saying, and it's absolutely one of the most important things you *can* say to a child (or anyone) today.

The very God who created us and our world says that there is a special future in front of us. Even with all the riots and wars and ruin and climate change around us, the reality of Jeremiah 29:11 remains true: "'For I know the plans that I have for you,' declares the LORD, 'plans . . . to give you a future and a hope.'"

Like all of God's Word, that statement is true! It doesn't mean there won't be trials and challenges. But if someone in your past or in your life today is saying with total certainty "There is no future!" that's a lie from the pit of hell. It's Satan who pushes death over life and curse over blessing.

God made us to be hope-dependent creatures.

It comes down to the fact that, according to the promises we have *in Christ*, the doomsayers are wrong! In even the most challenging situations, God made us to be *hope-dependent creatures*. All of us. Even in the worst of times or places.

When Hope and Life Are Erased All around Us

Viktor Frankl was a doctor and a prisoner at Auschwitz, the Nazi concentration camp. In his book called *Man's Search for Meaning* (which we strongly encourage you to read or listen to), he recounted how people could continue to live in the horrible, death-filled conditions at Auschwitz. What he found was that in order to survive, people need to believe in something.

Specifically, people needed to hang on to hope for the future.

If a man in Auschwitz kept believing there would come a time when the war ended—or that someday, sometime, he would be able to leave that horrible place and go see his family; or that he would again see a sunset that wasn't surrounded by barbed wire; or that he might eventually freely go to a market and sit and have coffee in the morning—if he held on to the hope that there was a future, he could endure the unendurable for one more day.

Time and again, however, someone would lose hope that there would be another day. For instance, Frankl wrote about a man who thought he knew (because of a dream) the exact day they would all be liberated from this death camp. The very thought filled this person with hope and energy. But then that date came and passed, and with its passing, the man lost any hope of a positive future. That, in turn, led to his quickly giving up hope and finally giving up on life altogether.

If you missed this element of the Blessing, we're not saying it's just because many people are pouring gasoline on our world and screaming to light the match. For most of us, it's a much more personal loss. It's the fact that *we don't believe there's a special future in front of us because we were told that* we *had no future or because our mistakes or decisions have cemented that lie in stone.*

Whatever reason the certainty of a special future has been robbed from you, know that there *is* a future and a hope. You can choose to look at life through the lens of the ultimate and in doing so be able to deal with the chaos of the immediate.

Did you receive or miss out on this fourth element of the Blessing?

One day while studying . . . I noticed there could be a relationship between chosen and redeemed. It seemed in my mind that these two words spoke of our value to God. I am so valuable to God that He still wanted me, even after He knew my whole life of sins that I would choose. He still wanted me! He would still redeem me from my slavery to sin. I am valuable to Him.

CARTER FEATHERSTON,
God Knows Your Story (and He's Not Mad!)

CHAPTER 8

WHEN WE MISS THE FIFTH ELEMENT: GENUINE COMMITMENT

You may think genuine commitment is nonexistent today. But it's not. You can see that in the example of late-night celebrity and car enthusiast Jay Leno. He was involved in a terrible car crash and severely burned. And then his wife, Mavis, became so deeply challenged by dementia that he had to take over conservatorship of all major decisions for her life. That's because tragically, she often doesn't know who her husband is or what's going on around her.

"People say marriage is difficult," Leno said recently at an award ceremony sponsored by his wife's foundation. "I don't get it. I enjoy her company. *I enjoy taking care of her.* We have fun. She's the most independent woman I ever knew. Again, I just couldn't be prouder of her."[1]

That's genuine commitment. Those are words from someone who knows there are trials and struggles—and still isn't going anywhere.

Did anyone demonstrate that kind of "I'm with you always!" commitment to you when you were growing up? Did you get that fifth element of the Blessing: *genuine commitment*?

The Red Paperboy Special

I (John) remember a Christmas story that taught me about this element of the Blessing. That story still has lessons for me today as I look back.

I was eleven years old, and all around me, life seemed to be falling apart in many ways. The slow wreck of our family had started the year before. My precious mother had gone from being a leading bank executive (a rarity for women back in the 1950s) to becoming physically disabled. In a blink, her body began to be ravaged by rheumatoid arthritis (RA).

Her hands were attacked first. They became so painful that she couldn't hold a pen and struggled to use a typewriter. Then her wrists and elbows became inflamed. By the end of that year, she was in such terrible pain that she had to take medical retirement.

At that stage in her fight against RA, she left our home in Arizona and traveled to Indiana. We had relatives there, including my Uncle Doc. He was a surgeon and could oversee her medical care. And there were other family members who loved her and could help care for her as well.

At eleven, from all the talk going on between the adults I'd overheard, I figured this was serious. I thought my mom would be gone for a *really* long time, like maybe even a month. But it was over two years before I'd see her again. Seemingly endless surgeries kept us apart.

In all, my mother would end up with two artificial ankles, two artificial hips, two artificial knees, and one artificial elbow replacement that didn't work. And all these surgical prostheses were *generations* behind the incredible implants available today. Those early models would break and keep adding to the incredibly painful mess her health had become.

My father was long gone from our lives. Now my mother was gone. And then at the start of that second year of my mother's surgeries, my twin brother was shipped back to Indiana. Finally, Joe, my older brother, was farmed out to a different aunt and uncle in Flagstaff, Arizona.

I didn't understand what was happening at the time. I wasn't aware that things had become so difficult financially that the adults were looking to cut expenses in every way they could. That meant spreading us boys out so there were fewer hungry mouths in one spot.

Which left Grandmother and me in our Arizona house.

Again, in large part because I didn't understand all that was happening, I was okay with farming everyone out. I was up for *anything* that might help my mother. Selfishly, too, with Christmas coming, I'm ashamed to say that in my eleven-year-old mind, it seemed logical that with everyone else gone, I would get more presents!

But in truth, there was only one present I wanted.

It was a glowing, shiny red 1959 Schwinn Paperboy Special bicycle. While Ralphie in *A Christmas Story* was desperate to get his hands on a Red Ryder BB gun, I had set my sights much higher.

That Paperboy Special was really called a Schwinn Wasp. From the moment I'd seen it at the bicycle store near us, I was in love. The bike was huge. The large whitewall tires made it look much taller than most bikes. And it was smothered with chrome accents. It had a chrome rack on the back *and* on the front along with chrome pedals and a red and white chrome chain protector. It also came with a huge chrome light mounted right in the middle of the handlebars—so big it looked like a car headlight!

Not to mention that incredibly cool black saddle seat, full of extra padding. And what nearly made me faint every time I saw it was another supercool accessory. Running the entire length of the frame, attached to the top tube (the long tube from the handlebars to the seat), they'd added something that looked like a gas tank you'd see on a motorcycle! It was heart-stopping for an eleven-year-old. Everything and more that a paperboy could think or dream about was there in candy-apple red.

Certainly, I left enough hints everywhere for my grandmother. She couldn't miss that I only wanted that one small, simple gift for Christmas. After all, there were only the two of us now. I knew things were tough, but I was doing everything I could to help out. I got up at the crack of dawn before school to throw a paper route—that I would soon be doing on my new Wasp.

Perhaps the most difficult thing to deal with was Scott, a classmate who lived down the street. He wasn't a paperboy, but he already rode a beautiful blue Newsboy Special manufactured by Schwinn's rival, Columbia. It was more expensive than the Schwinn. But then again, his father owned a cotton gin. So money for things like bicycles wasn't an issue in his home.

What was an issue to me was how often Scott would *just happen* to ride that blue beauty by me and wave. This as I was trudging by on my paper route.

But again, as beautiful as his bike was, I didn't bother with any bike envy. His bike was blue, for heaven's sake. Not bright red like my Paperboy Special would be. And I knew that Christmas was almost here.

Christmas Eve finally arrived. Grandmother outdid herself making turkey, dressing, green beans cooked with bacon, and homemade mashed potatoes with loads of gravy. She also made two kinds of pies for only the two of us, both of them buttery and perfectly baked—her famous strawberry rhubarb pie and her cherry pie with sugar-coated crust *and ice cream.*

It was a feast. And I didn't have to share my favorite piece of anything with anyone. After dinner, I just lazed around for the rest of the evening, waiting to be outside on my new bike the next morning. I was already picturing how Scott would *just happen* to ride by, as he always did, to tell me about all he'd gotten that year.

When I walked down the hall later that evening, my grandmother was in her room . . . *crying.* I went in to try to understand what had happened, hoping she hadn't just gotten bad news from Indiana about Mom or someone else in the family.

She pulled me into a hug, sobbing, and said, "I'm so sorry."

I wondered, *What in the world could she be sorry for?* It had been a perfect Christmas Eve.

That's when she told me, "We just ate your Christmas present."

And as she held me, it began to dawn on me that all the money she'd had for Christmas had just gone into that feast. *Not into a bike.*

There would be no presents that year. No bike nor anything else. I thought the small plastic Christmas tree she'd put up didn't have presents under it because a bike wouldn't fit. Now I knew the real reason.

That's when she told me, "We just ate your Christmas present."

It was the only time in my life when I haven't received way more than enough Christmas presents. Instead, that Christmas, we both sat on Grandmother's small single bed and cried.

Genuine Commitment and the Christmas Story

After what seemed like forever of being sad, we both finally pulled ourselves together. And Grandmother pulled out her Bible (which she did often during those days).

We sat together, and she read us the Christmas story. Of God coming down to earth. Of angels on high declaring peace on earth and goodwill toward men. And that was one of those moments when almighty God's love and blessing, His holding me tight along with my grandmother in those toughest of times for us, broke into my world.

And life was never the same.

There was no mom at home that Christmas. No twin or older brother to play with that night or all day the next. No presents. No red bike. But as I sat with my grandmother, who hugged me and was there for me, I knew the almighty God was sitting right there with me as well.

This was long before I knew anything about how genuine commitment is a major part of the biblical blessing or about its major role in attachment science. But in that moment on my grandmother's bed, God broke through to teach me about genuine commitment. In that moment, I knew she wasn't going anywhere. And even if our family had to be apart, they weren't going anywhere really. They were just holding on to me from afar.

And I knew as well that I had God's immense, strong, gentle arms around me. I knew His love was unshakable and unending and there really was such a thing as genuine commitment. I'd seen it up close and personal, Grandma's love reflecting God's.

And yes, the next morning, Scott did just happen to ride his bike by our house. He even stopped and invited me over to his house. We spent Christmas Day having a blast, playing with all the incredible toys and games he'd gotten. But all day I felt as if I'd already received *way* more than Scott for Christmas.

That's a long story to bring you to a short question: *Did you receive this fifth element of the Blessing growing up?*

Did your parents or other loved ones give you a commitment that seemed to you unshakable, both in happy days and in challenging ones? Or is the thing you look back on how easily or often commitments could be broken? Promises made but not kept—like the times you were told "Your father will be coming over on Saturday" and he never showed up.

From True Security to Self-Protection

What is perhaps the most difficult thing about missing genuine commitment is the way it pushes us toward self-protection. When we're young, most of us have not been taught to deal with pain.

Instead of working through it in a healthy way, we often find something that *seems* to cover it.

For example, Jackson grew up extremely short and heavy at a time when bullying wasn't frowned upon but was just part of life. Then came the summer before his seventh-grade year. He grew almost two inches over the summer. In the next several years, he grew more inches. By freshman year, he had discovered weight lifting. By his senior year, he was six foot three and 245 pounds, and he could bench-press more than 300 pounds! No one bullied him anymore! He was now an all-city football offensive guard.

> *They constructed public selves that looked good— until they didn't or couldn't anymore.*

But here came the problem: Jackson had found something that he thought would help with all his pain from being picked on and missing any kind of blessing at home. He could just keep lifting weights. He could get a football scholarship. He could become so big and tough that no one would pick on him.

Then, in the first play of his first game senior year, a blindside block broke his arm and irreparably ruined his knee. His football career was over, his scholarship offer was withdrawn, and his life fell apart.

For Mariah, her incredible intelligence provided a sense of self-protection. Then she got older, and even with all her brilliance, she was replaced at work by someone younger who would work for less money.

Then there was Ben, who was great at making money. But he discovered that while he could buy all the things he wanted, none of them would protect him from the pain of missing the Blessing in childhood.

What all of them had to do was finally come to grips with what we call *image management*. That's where someone tries to keep up a public self that says "Everything's great!" but ignores any private hurts or realities. Jackson, Mariah, and Ben had all found something external that they thought they could build their lives on. They constructed public selves that looked good—until they didn't or couldn't anymore. And that's when they were forced to deal with those private-self issues they'd tried never to face, like missing the Blessing and never finding hope or healing. Without the security of knowing someone is holding us—committed to us—we're wide open to image management.

Genuine commitment is a gift, modeled first by God, that can't be taken from us. It's a huge part of what we all need and receive when we get the Blessing. It's a major part of our emotional struggles when we don't.

Did you miss it? It's not a minor loss. It's a huge one. But don't give up hope. Such commitment is just a few chapters away.

We've looked now at these five elements of the Blessing through the lens of what happens when we miss them. It's time to think about your pictures, your memories. Which ones did you receive? Which were withheld from you? What feelings, what dreams, what pictures of missing them come to the surface?

No home is perfect. No parents are perfect. Certainly not our homes. But before we go on, think over those elements that were present or absent in your past. And in doing so, make special note of one last thing:

There is so much hope and help coming.

Please keep that in mind, and don't put down this book. It may not be easy to look at the elements of the Blessing you've missed. *But know that when we're done with this section, there's so much positive ahead.*

You can discover how to turn wrongs around. To reverse the curse. To add back those spoken words and high value and that picture of a special future and genuine commitment—even appropriate, meaningful touch—can be yours to give and live.

So think about your pictures, your memories, but keep on going. The picture is going to get much brighter.

Did You Receive or Miss These Elements of the Blessing?

Appropriate, Meaningful Touch
Spoken Words
Attaching High Value
Picturing a Special Future
Genuine Commitment

I cried to the LORD in my trouble,

And He answered me.

PSALM 120:1

CHAPTER 9

HOMES THAT WITHHOLD THE BLESSING

We've gone through the five elements of the Blessing. Each one is biblically based and a much-needed relational building block on the positive side of attachment. But if missed, each can become the source of a lot of hurt and our deep cry to be blessed.

We've seen now how blessing and curse are linked with the choice for life or death (Deuteronomy 30:19). It turns out that that's not an exaggeration, spiritually or relationally.

In an eye-opening study out of UNC–Chapel Hill, researchers are learning how a child's *life expectancy* is linked to his or her relationship with caregivers and other significant influences![1] Drawing on research from four major studies on health and longevity in children, researchers found that a *lack* of close-knit, face-to-face relationships is actively linked with high blood pressure, abdominal obesity, heart disease, stroke, and even cancer risk. Conversely, the risk of these all negative physical measures can *go down* as you help your child experience and learn how to build loving, close-knit relationships.

And at the heart of building that beneficial connectedness are those five elements of giving and living out the Blessing! Those same elements are central to *emotional* health as well.

Another recent study on childhood memories found that *the memories most often linked with a happy childhood* did not involve how many major vacations or experiences parents provided for their children. Nor were they linked with the number of *things* they were given. Being happy in childhood wasn't even linked to the absence of negative or difficult experiences. Instead, emotional happiness was linked to the very same thing that affects physical health: *the degree of connected, caring relationships in the home.*[2]

In short, research affirms the importance of each element of the Blessing!

That's why it's important to understand what the *absence* of the Blessing looks like in a home, especially if you were raised in one that lacked it.

A Warning Label before We Walk into These Homes

What if you grew up in a home that withheld the Blessing?

Before we begin our tour of these homes and their common characteristics, we want to make two things clear. First, it's not easy to look at hurtful homes. However, looking back is often an essential part of healing and then moving forward. Denial and image management lead to depression, not rest for our souls.

Second, our goal with this chapter is to bring to light things that can help you heal, not to add another layer of anger or bitterness to an already-strained relationship. Nor would we have you blame all present problems on the past or on the actions of others.

In fact, we hope the opposite is true. By honestly looking at these homes, you'll realize that, in most cases, parents or other significant persons who never gave you the Blessing never received it themselves! For many, there were factors that weighed greatly in blocking their blessing of others. The horrors of war, mental challenges, or abuse in the past are some examples of things that may leave a person unable or unwilling to bless.

No Excuse for Bad Behavior

My (John's) father was an angry alcoholic. I worked hard to understand how the war and his non-blessing family background had ruined him in many ways. For example, just watch the World War II series by Steven Spielberg and Tom Hanks called *The Pacific*. Note especially the episode focused on the battle at Peleliu Island. That was *one place* my father fought. No wonder he came home hating everything and everyone, trying and failing to drink away all the terrible pictures and pain he'd seen.

I certainly honor his service and grieve that he came home so broken. But I still never let our kids get in the car with him. I never dropped appropriate boundaries, but I also know that the biblical word for *forgiveness* means "to untie the knot."

When I hated my father, *I* was the one tied up in knots. After I came to Christ, I tried to learn more about him. I didn't want to be all tied up in knots from what had not been in my life.

When I hated my father, I was the one tied up in knots.

In short, seeking to understand our pasts and whether we missed the Blessing shouldn't lead to more hate or seeking harm. Our prayer is that as we look at these homes, some things will happen that only God can do. First, you'll realize that once you get God's blessing, you can begin to give it to others—even (in a healthy way) bless someone who never gave it to you. In some cases, you might reverse years of curse with blessing.

Second, if you do find yourself in the pictures of any of these five homes, there will come a moment when God breaks through for you and, in Christ, you find the freedom to move on.

Consider Helen's story.

"I Know You Did Your Best, Mom."

Helen is a wonderful woman in her seventies who signed up for one of our *The Blessing* Zoom book clubs. As that particular club started, all of us learned that Helen was a new Christian. It was also obvious she was from New York City. She was born and had spent all her life in the city, complete with that wonderful accent and attitude to match.

As the weeks went by, in the breakout groups and in the larger group, we also learned that Helen came from an extremely hurtful home. Her mother had suffered from severe mental issues. A lot of hurt had been passed on to Helen day after day. Never once in her childhood did she receive any element of the Blessing from anyone in her home.

But Helen was faithful in showing up each week. She read *The Blessing*. She asked questions and took part in the discussions—until she got to one section toward the end of the book.

It was a section where Kari had written several blessings people could say out loud over themselves, particularly if they'd missed the Blessing. Each line is right out of Scripture and a clear picture of how God looks at us in love.

There were about twenty people in our last book club meeting. Helen raised her hand (via the Zoom emoji) and said she wanted to say something.

"Yesterday, I read the part of the book with the list where you're supposed to read over yourself a list of things to bless yourself. I read the first thing on the list: 'You are loved.' Then I read the second thing: 'You are wanted.'"

There was a long pause.

When she finally gathered herself, she said in a shaky voice, "And then I cried for almost three hours. For the first time in my life, I believed those words. God really does want me. And others do too."

As she wept that night, I don't think there was one of us on that Zoom call who wasn't crying with her. All of us were sorry for the incredible pain she'd suffered. All of us were rejoicing and grateful for how God had used something so small—just three words, *You are wanted*—to change her life deeply.

Most of us had read those same words in that assigned chapter. Perhaps they had caused a few to nod their heads. But most of us had read right through them or even skipped over that section.

But what a beautiful example of what we mean about those *moments* in our lives. The ones that wake us up from the bad dream. Those moments that—only because of God's Spirit and love—convince us we really are worthy of being blessed by our Lord and others. We pray you will experience such moments through this book.

We stopped right then and prayed for Helen. That gave her a chance to gather herself even more. And that's when she said something even more incredible.

"I probably shouldn't share this. I don't know how you feel about dreams. I'm not sure how *I* feel about them. But after crying so long, I went to bed last night, and I had a dream. And my mother was there."

She had told us earlier that her mother had passed away several years before.

"I purposely haven't thought about her for years. It was just too painful. But I went right up to her, and I hugged her. I told her that I loved her and that I forgave her."

And then she ended, *"And I told her she had done the best she could. I had never said that to my mother."*

We all realized it was a dream, but what an amazing picture of forgiveness! And how kind of the Lord to provide that much-needed moment for her in a way that meant so much. That was made possible only by God's forgiveness in her life and then His love breaking through to her as she looked at her broken past.

Only through God's love and grace can we honestly look at our parents and our pasts and find the freedom we need to forgive and change the pictures—to be truly free to leave that hurt in a healthy way and cleave to others in present relationships (see Genesis 2:24).

Our goal, then, in looking at homes that withhold the Blessing is to better understand our own and our parents' backgrounds, including how our parents were influenced by *their* parents.

Dr. Brie Turns-Coe is an outstanding therapist and friend who leads the marriage and family therapy master's program at Arizona Christian University. She has also written an outstanding book called *Parent the Child You Have, Not the Child You Were.*[3] Ouch. For many of us, just that title is enough to remind us how we are affected by what's happened to us.

Only through God's love and grace can we honestly look at our parents and our pasts and find the freedom we need to forgive and change the pictures.

We simply can't out-hate what's happened in our pasts. It freezes us right back in the place we've tried so hard to escape from. And yes, it's easy to look at our children and see them only through the lens of what we've experienced. But it's time to look back in a way that helps us choose life and freedom, and that frees our children from our being frozen in the past.

It's time we start moving toward God's best, to become people of blessing with His help. That wasn't easy for Helen, and it won't be easy for us. But our prayer is that like Helen, as you read about these homes and the rest of this book, you'll have your own moment of healing.

The First Home: Facing a Flood or a Drought

In the spring and summertime, the Seattle–Tacoma area where I (Kari) live is particularly beautiful. It's lush and green. Almost every day for months starting in October and lasting through May, clouds roll in and drench the cities around the Puget Sound. But finally, around late June, just when we're all thinking the rain will never end—and I start begging my husband, Joey, to move back to Arizona—the sun comes out. And for several months, the green and growth are spectacular.

If you travel a few hours inland and east, however, you'll run into one of our favorite places to hike, camp, and explore: the Cascade Range. These breathtaking mountains are so effective at halting the rain from the coast that few clouds get past them. As a result, the land on the eastern side of Washington is actually semiarid.

We can see a similar phenomenon in many homes today. For any number of reasons, one child will be drenched with lush showers of blessing from his or her parents. As a result, outwardly this child thrives and grows.

Unfortunately, sitting "just east" of him or her at the dinner table can be one or more siblings whose emotional lives are like parched ground. So few drops of blessing have fallen on the soil of their lives that emotional cracks begin to form. This phenomenon is as old as the Bible.

We've already read about Jacob receiving the Blessing and his brother missing it. After Jacob grew up and had children of his own, we see that one child got showers of blessing and the others mere drops:

> Now Israel [Jacob] loved Joseph more than all his other sons, because he was the son of his old age; and he made him a multicolored tunic. And his brothers saw that their father loved him more than all his brothers; and so they hated him and could not speak to him on friendly terms.
> GENESIS 37:3-4

That beautiful tunic may have spelled special acceptance to one son, but it brought out hatred from eleven brothers. Each brother knew he was living without something Joseph had received. And his brothers' anger reached such proportions that they came close to putting him to death (see Genesis 37:18-22).

Does unfiltered, undisguised favoritism sound like your home growing up?

Consider Jade and her brother, Jordan. Jade was not merely showered with the Blessing from her father; she was flooded with it! Her father paid so much attention to her that he rarely spoke words of blessing to her mother or her older sibling, Jordan.

Jade and Jordan's parents had struggled in their marriage for some time. In fact, getting pregnant with Jade had been a last-ditch attempt by their mother to keep the relationship together.

At first, this seemed to work well. Their marriage was better than it had been in years. But as the children grew older, problems began to creep back into the marriage. Sadly, Jade's father began turning away from his wife and focused all his attention on Jade as a form of escape.

As more "rain" fell on Jade, how did Jordan respond? Like Joseph's brothers, he was angry at being almost ignored. And like many we work with who faced extreme favoritism and missed the Blessing, Jordan also carried a nagging sense of insecurity about whether he was truly valuable as a person, or even worthy to be loved. From trips that Dad planned just for himself and Jade to places like Disneyland, Europe, and beyond to continual comments about never really wanting a son, Jordan suffered as he was reminded often that he would never be enough for his father.

Perhaps surprisingly, Jordan wasn't the only one hurting. Jade also struggled with all the focus and blessing poured on her. Her father smothered her with so much attention that boys her own age paled in comparison. Her father even acted like a jealous rival when she started dating, pointing out every flaw he could see in her young men.

Instead of preparing her to leave home and cleave to a spouse in a healthy way, that deluge of attention blocked Jade from building healthy attachment bonds with her mother, with friends, or with anyone else. She also struggled whenever the spotlight shone on someone other than her!

Jade was insecure as well. When others didn't seem to value her as much as her father did, she acted out, desperate to get the same level of love and affection from them. As she grew into adulthood, this unhealthy behavior led to destructive friendships and romantic relationships and even an ongoing battle with addiction.

In other words, both kinds of children—those who are smothered with the Blessing and those who have it withheld from them—can struggle when coming from a home of favoritism.

The Second Home: Where the Blessing Is Placed Just out of Reach

Rachel spent her life in a home where, no matter how hard she tried or how much she accomplished, the Blessing was always moved just out of reach. Both her mother and father demanded excellence before offering any kind words or affirmation.

To try to get her parents' blessing, Rachel studied extremely hard. But every A on her report card should have been an A+. And every academic achievement—even graduating magna cum laude—should have been just a little bit better. To quote her mom, "If magna was good, summa was better."

In addition, to get her father's blessing, Rachel worked hard to become an outstanding athlete, just like he'd been. She won state in several events in track and field, led her team to a state softball victory, and even received a full-ride scholarship to play volleyball at a prestigious university. But her father's responses mirrored her mother's. Every achievement was just short of earning his pride and his blessing.

After college, where she succeeded in surpassing her mother's GPA and her father's athletic achievements, she met and married a wonderful man named Colin. Colin was kind, loving, a strong believer, successful at his job, and crazy about Rachel.

However, Colin still wasn't wonderful enough for Rachel's parents.

Every family event, holiday, or birthday became an excuse for them to remind her she could have done better. During visits to Rachel's home, her mother would point out the couple's second-hand vintage furniture (that both Rachel and Colin loved) or Rachel's well-worn outfits as a way of reminding her daughter that she and Colin still weren't enough.

Then, a few years later, Rachel and Colin had two beautiful boys. And Rachel watched in horror as her parents turned their withholding on her children as well.

It was one thing to feel she could never live up to her parents' expectations or receive their blessing, but it was a completely different layer of pain to watch her children try to experience their grandparents' love and find it always just out of reach.

Can you see how that deep desire for the Blessing became like an everyday living tug-of-war for Rachel? She was pulled one direction to try to please her parents, even though what they wanted for her wasn't what she wanted. And she was pulled another direction to try to enjoy the incredible life she and Colin had built. The pressure was constant. It not only affected her joy and the way she viewed herself, but it was also putting stress on her marriage and now her children, too.

The best part of working with Rachel and Colin was the freedom she finally found to move away from that exhausting search for the Blessing that was ruining many positive things in her life! Can you relate to a home with an always-out-of-reach blessing?

The Third Home: When a Tradition Robs You of the Blessing

Isaiah was almost twenty-one. He was a senior in college and home on winter break. He had one spring semester to go, and then graduation and next steps into life after school. And Isaiah felt sure he knew where God was leading him.

That certainty, however, was at the center of why he was confused and brokenhearted. He had been a model son. *And now he had been put out of his house by his father!*

He hadn't just been told to leave. Every stitch of clothing and personal effects in what had been his room had been tossed outside onto the carport. And his parents had made it clear that it would all be thrown away the next day if he didn't take it away. He was no longer welcome to live there.

What had caused such a rift? Certainly, it had to be something heinous and evil. Maybe open rebellion? Lying? Stealing?

For Isaiah's parents, it was something worse.

There was a *tradition* in his family. And if you were going to receive the Blessing in that home, you had better keep that tradition.

Isaiah's father was a minister. His grandfather was a minister. Even his great-grandfather had been in ministry. Three generations of Smiths had heard the call to full-time spiritual service early in life and had unquestioningly responded.

Isaiah had become a Christian when he was young, and he had grown in his love for the Lord over the years. He had already spent almost four full years at a top-notch Christian college. He was seriously dating a pastor's daughter.

In every way, he was on a journey that looked as if it would take him right to the kind of choices and future that had been programmed into him from generations past. Certainly seminary would be next and then a pastorate to continue the legacy.

But on the night he'd ended up on the street, Isaiah had told his parents of a different decision he said he'd made after much prayer and thought, and he was asking for their support.

He had decided to pursue a career in marketing, not ministry.

He truly felt he could serve the Lord best in the business world and still do ministry as a lay leader. And as he talked, he handed his parents his acceptance letter into an outstanding MBA program.

Isaiah thought they'd be excited for him.

He was terribly wrong.

The anger was immediate and nearly overwhelming. At first, his parents pounced on his girlfriend, whom they accused of luring Isaiah away from his calling. That must be it. She resented growing up poor in a pastor's home, and now she didn't want to face life on another pastor's salary. But that proved to be false. She was all in on Isaiah's going either into ministry or marketing.

So his closest friends who were believers must be at fault. But it turned out they hadn't pushed him away from the family tradition either.

No, it came down to Isaiah himself. And as he explained that he had personally sought God's wisdom and direction, it became personal all right. It was a personal affront to his parents, who had just lost generational bragging rights going back decades. Someone in their lineage had broken the family tradition. In their minds, that someone needed to pay.

In this sad example—and many others we've seen—parents who withhold the Blessing feel they've been cheated out of something they expect from their children. They expect (demand) their son to come back and run the family business, for example. Only he doesn't, and he loses their blessing by not following that tradition.

In another case, a woman's siblings all lived not just in the same state but in the same city, and all within a few miles of their parents. So when she announced that she and her husband were moving out of state—with the only grandchildren—there went another tradition and her blessing.

These are not parents who struggle with the very real and tragic need to cut off contact with a prodigal child for a season. These parents cut off all communication over how someone votes or after finding out who they've donated money to or after discovering they've just bought a gas car instead of an EV. These are parents who, out of anger, are not trying to do what's best for a child; they are intentionally causing harm by choosing to cut off all kindness. There's no bending, no discussion beyond arguments that their child needs to quit doing "wrong" or even "sinning" and get back in line with the family's tradition. There's no willingness to abide differences that have nothing to do with sin or rebellion.

They are intentionally causing harm by choosing to cut off all kindness.

If you grew up in a home like this and decide to travel a different road, you'll find no shelter, blessing, or acceptance. You can expect winter followed by winter followed by more cold shoulders for you and your children and grandchildren.

The Fourth Home: Where You Receive a Part of the Blessing

My (John's) parents divorced when I was only a couple of months old. I would spend years longing for my father's blessing. I'll tell more of this story in the next section of the book.

Our mother was doing a world-class job of giving me and my brothers each element of the Blessing. It's not that she could or should have done more to try to make up for the hurt I felt. My pain came from the missing parent, from my father who was never there.

Those like me who got only a part of the Blessing can experience one set of problems, like the idealization of the missing parent. (*One day I'll meet him, and things will finally be right.*) I lived that out. Or the opposite can happen. If the parent who stays with the children makes the one who left the sole villain, there are no two sides to what happened. There's no one standing up for the parent who is being cut down (which, in some cases, is absolutely justified).

We've met with a number of people who have struggled with missing the Blessing from an absent mother or father but then finally met the other person and heard a different side of the story. The result is often a very real disconnect, even resentment toward the parent who stayed.

In my case, my mother did a good job of not putting down my father. My animosity toward him grew on its own as she grew sicker. As things got worse in every way, there was never any contact or help from him (child support, for example).

But for other people, their partial blessing is much more pronounced and hurtful. For example, there are children who spend one week at one parent's home and then pack up and spend one week at the other's. They split vacations and holidays. That can work when both parents are healthy, helpful, and honoring of each other. But what often happens is that one week is spent in a solidly loving, blessing-based, healthy home. Then the next week, the kids are bundled off to drugs, sex, and rock and roll. Then it's back to a place of stability. And then back to a place where chaos reigns. The result? Damage is inflicted emotionally, relationally, and spiritually.

It's challenging to try to live in both light and darkness. In one place, Jesus is honored and the Blessing is given. That home is full of safety, health, and appropriate boundaries. But in the other home, Jesus' name is constantly used as an expletive or mocking joke. Chaos is the norm. And nothing is stable, safe, or healthy. In many ways, I think I (John) had it easier.

Certainly, it was a huge loss to never have had a father growing up. But it can be much more difficult, and much more confusing, if children go from blessing to curse and back again all through their growing-up years.

The Fifth Home: Where the Blessing Is Exchanged for a Burden

Finally, in some homes that withhold the Blessing, there's a counterfeit form of blessing that comes too often at a terrible price. Read the words of one woman who expressed her pain to a national columnist. Her words speak of an incredible cost associated with gaining only a small part of a real blessing:

> Ever since I was a little girl, my mother made me feel guilty if I did not do exactly as she wanted. Dozens of times she has said, "You will be sorry when I am in my coffin." I was never a bad girl. I always did everything she requested me to do. . . .
>
> Both my parents are eighty-two. One of these days my mother will die, and I am terrified of what it will do to me.[4]

This poor woman paid a tremendous price for her blessing—a lifetime of trying to please her mother. Yet even now she's not even sure she received her mother's blessing! Despite all her efforts, there's great fear that after all that, she'll be left with a burden, not a blessing.

Did you grow up in a home where, through guilt or fear, you were coaxed or shamed or threatened into giving up your rights or goals or future to get some kind of counterfeit blessing?

The Blessing in Scripture was never meant to be earned. It doesn't come with threats or strings attached. It doesn't come with the massive burden of having to keep a terrible secret like the one Nicole was given.

When Nicole was only nine years old, her parents divorced. After a whirlwind romance, her mother remarried in under six months, and a stepfather moved into the house. When Nicole's mother was away at work one evening, her stepfather came into her room. What started out as playing became an evening of shame and horror for Nicole. Like thousands of young girls, she became the victim of sexual abuse.

The next morning, her stepfather pulled Nicole aside and told her that if she ever mentioned to anyone what had happened, he would divorce her mother, beat her mother up, and leave both of them to starve on the street. On the other hand, if she told no one, he would be nice to her and her mother.

The fear of what would happen to her and her mother plus her feelings of shame kept Nicole quiet. Because she never mentioned to her mother what had happened, her stepfather kept his part of the bargain. He went on with his life and marriage as though nothing had ever happened. He even treated her decently after that terrible evening.

But in remaining quiet to keep her stepfather's favor, Nicole paid a terrible price. As long as she lived there, she was emotionally held hostage in her own home. In error, she believed her silence would buy her stepfather's blessing for her and her mother. Only later did she realize that a man like her stepfather gives only a curse or a blessing that's counterfeit.

When we first met Nicole, she was married and the mother of three children. For years she had been living in another state and only infrequently saw her mother. Unable to reveal her deepest hurt, she heard those painful memories shout to her day and night. Only when she finally shared her secret with her loving husband and sought help did she begin to find freedom from this past burden. (She also tried and failed to press charges against her stepfather.)

Do you relate to a home life like Nicole's, where a burden was given rather than a blessing? If you see your own experience in any of these five homes that withhold blessing, you know the same pain we've lived with. But remember, *the good news is coming*. Before we get to that in the next part of the book, however, we need to ask, *What do we become if we're raised in a home without the Blessing?*

Without the Blessing, We Can Become . . .

The Seekers

We've looked at several examples of children who reacted to missing the Blessing by beginning a lifelong search. Seekers are always searching for intimacy but seldom able to tolerate it. These people feel tremendous fulfillment in the thrill of courtship. But after marriage, their lack of acceptance from their parents leaves them uncomfortable in receiving it from a spouse. Never sure of how acceptance feels, they are never satisfied with holding it too long. Because of the lack of permanence in the Blessing in their early lives, they can even struggle to believe in God's unchanging love for them.

The Shattered

These people are deeply troubled over the lack of their parents' love and acceptance. Fear, anxiety, depression, and emotional withdrawal can often be traced to a person's missing out on his or her family's blessing. This unhappy road can even lead a person to consider whether life is worth living.

The Needy

Like two-thousand-pound sponges, these folks react to missing their parents' blessing by sucking every bit of life and energy from a spouse, child, friend, or entire church congregation. They are left so emotionally empty that they latch onto other people with their unmet needs and, like parasites, drain others of their emotional energy.

Unfortunately, when other people—trying to make up for years of unmet needs—finally tire of carrying the entire emotional weight of them, the message the needy receive is that they're being rejected. Deeply hurt once again, they never realize that they've brought this pain upon themselves. They end up pushing away the blessing other people offer when they actually desperately need it.

The Angry

As long as people are angry at each other, they are chained to each other emotionally. Many adults are still emotionally chained to their parents because they're angry after missing the Blessing. They have never forgiven nor forgotten. As a result, the rattle and chafing of emotional chains distract them from intimacy in other relationships. Many people thus go into adult life with chips on their shoulders put there early, when they believed they could never experience love and acceptance in their homes.

The Detached

An old proverb says, "Once burned, twice shy." This motto is used by some children who have missed out on the Blessing. Having never received it from an important person in their lives once, they spend a lifetime protecting themselves from letting that disappointment ever happen again. They keep their spouses, children, and close friends at arm's length to protect themselves. The heavy price is inviting loneliness to take up residence in their lives.

The Driven

In this category we find extreme perfectionists, workaholics, the notoriously picky, and generally demanding people who pursue their blessing the old-fashioned way: They try to "earn it." The only problem is that the Blessing is a gift. You cannot buy, earn, or manipulate it. You can find some counterfeit blessings for sale—at a terrible price—but they last only as long as the showroom shine on a new car. Such counterfeit blessings rust and corrode once they leave the dealership. Missing their parents' blessing challenges these driven people to attack an accomplishment in an illusory attempt to gain love, acceptance, and—even harder to grasp—rest for their souls.

The Seduced

Many people who have missed out on their parents' blessing look for that lost love in all the wrong places. Unhealthy coping mechanisms abound as they attempt to meet legitimate needs in illegitimate ways. Sex, porn, substance abuse, and eating disorders are just a few examples. All too often, these people pick up a drink or take a pill to try to cover up the hurt from empty relationships in the past or present. Addiction and other forms of self-medicating can become counterfeits for the deep emotional warmth of experiencing the elements of the Blessing.

For example, a recent study of compulsive gamblers with pathological gambling addictions found they are more likely to have suffered childhood traumas, including physical abuse or witnessing violence in the home.[5]

Can You Really Change the Pictures of Your Life Story?

Here we are then, midway through the book, and you've learned about the five elements of the Blessing through the lens of having missed them. And you've seen what can happen in five common types of homes that withhold the Blessing.

Is there really a way out when your hurt was in the past? How do you go back and change the pictures of your life story? Is it even possible to move from a life of curse to one full of blessing?

That's exactly what we believe can happen in the next section, as we share with you our own journeys of moving from missing the Blessing to finding a way forward. The negative pictures your heart remembers don't have to control you. You really can learn to receive, give, and live the Blessing.

PART TWO

PERSONAL PICTURES OF REVERSING THE CURSE

You know, we just don't recognize the most significant moments of our lives while they're happening. Back then I thought, well, there'll be other days. I didn't realize that that was the only day.

DR. ARCHIBALD "MOONLIGHT" GRAHAM,
Field of Dreams

CHAPTER 10

"IT'S YOUR DAD"

What would you rather have if you landed in a new city, a map or a guide? That's what this second part of the book is all about. As we begin the process of reversing the curse and changing the pictures of your life story, we first want to be your trusted guides and share *our* stories with you. In different ways, we had to move through those same stages you're moving through if you missed the Blessing. So here we'll walk you through our stories of missing, receiving, giving, and living the Blessing with those we love.

We know those first steps can be very hard. So, in this next section, you can walk alongside us in our failures and see God showing up to bring change. We hope that will reinforce the fact that you *can* change. You can move past missing the Blessing.

But we want to give you a choice. Maybe you feel like you don't need a guide and are ready to jump into the seven steps toward healing we outline in the next section. If so, feel free to jump to chapter 16. If, however, our stories of having been there and come out on the other side will be encouraging to you, read on.

Whether you're skipping ahead or you're about to walk through our journeys with us, we pray you'll find the light you need for your path—the one that moves you from curse to blessing, from death to life.

John's Story

For decades now, the movie *Field of Dreams* has had a powerful effect on a lot of people, myself (John) included.[1] The story is about a lot of things. Baseball. Nostalgia. America's past. But most of all, it's about the healing of memories.

On one level, it's about the healing of a professional wound left behind when eight White Sox players were banned from baseball for conspiring to throw the 1919 World Series. On another level, it's about the healing of a relational wound left behind when a father was taken out of his son's life by dying suddenly.

The son's mother had died when he was three, leaving his father to raise him. The son had some good memories of his father, like being put to bed with stories of Babe Ruth, Lou Gehrig, and Shoeless Joe Jackson; being taken to baseball games; and playing catch. But as the boy grew up, other memories overshadowed those. Memories of disagreements and arguments and of leaving home in rebellion.

The father died a few years after the son had experienced the '60s at Berkeley, graduated, and gotten married. Along with some deep-seated resentment, there was regret for words that were spoken—and for those that never were. What was left in the son's heart was an ache, a longing for one more game of catch. For a conversation. For a relationship.

The movie opens with a montage of memories—old photograph albums, home movies, and single pictures that highlight the past. The first picture in the album is a close-up of a boy in coveralls. As the now-adult boy tells his story through pictures and voice-over, the camera pulls back to reveal the boy sitting cross-legged in a field.

The boy was born in 1952, the same year I was.

The next picture is neatly matted—a soldier standing in a doorway somewhere in France during World War I. He's young and lean, sharply dressed in his uniform. He looks every bit a hero, at least in the eyes of that cross-legged little boy.

When I was that boy's age, the fields I sat in, played in, and dreamed in were the slopes of Camelback Mountain in Phoenix, Arizona. That's where my brothers and I played army, challenging other neighborhoods to war. On that battlefield, we built forts, planned ambushes, and set booby traps. With dirt clods as hand grenades, along with our imaginary bazookas, machine guns, and a volley of sound effects, we fought the enemy.

On those fields we lived out our dream of being heroes.

It was a great place to grow up. Neighborhoods were safe, playmates were plentiful, and summer days stretched forever.

That kid I once was grew up never knowing his father. He left when I was two months old. He left a wife and three small boys. He left her to bathe us, feed us, and clothe us. Left her to nurse us when we were sick, tutor us when we couldn't understand our homework, and discipline us when we got out of line. He left her to provide for us, protect us, and point us in the right direction.

That kid I once was grew up never knowing his father.

If anyone was ever equal to such a task, it was my mom. Her name was Zoa. It means "life." Her mother meant to call her Zoe, which is a much more common name and spelling. But this was 1920. Her mother handwrote her birth certificate and misspelled her name! So, officially and legally, Zoa she would be. And she gave so much life to each of us.

I never heard her speak negatively about my dad. But she never spoke candidly about him either. If his name ever came up in conversation, she only said, "Mom and Dad don't live together anymore." She never said why. And she never assessed blame.

I don't remember missing my father, at least in those early

years. How can you miss something you've never had? Someone you've never known? I grew up not knowing what he looked or sounded like, how tall he was or what color hair he had. There were no pictures of him in the house. Not on the walls. Not on the bookshelves. Not even in the scrapbooks.

Then one day, when bored and rummaging through the house for a game, I opened one of my mother's drawers. In the drawer was a sheaf of papers, and their oldness intrigued me. The yellowing newsprint. The mustiness of another era. The crumbling mystery of it all. As a boy with a rich fantasy life, I was certain I had stumbled upon something important. Treasure maps, maybe. Coded messages. Who knows what secrets were hidden there?

Leafing through the pages of my mother's past, I found a picture that had been scissored out of an Anderson, Indiana, newspaper. The man in the picture was a soldier, dressed in combat fatigues, and a captain or general or someone important was pinning a medal on him in the field.

The picture mesmerized me. Maybe it was because it was 1958 and pictures of soldiers still lived on the battlefields of our black-and-white TV. Maybe it was because I was a boy who loved storming the hills of Camelback Mountain. Or maybe it was something deep inside, an inarticulate ache for something I never had. I don't know.

I took it to my mom. "Who's this?" I asked.

She took the picture in her hand, pausing a moment. She looked at me, returned the picture, and then, as if she knew this moment would one day come, said, "It's your dad."

She told me that the picture was taken after the Battle of Guadalcanal and that he was receiving a field decoration for bravery. The eighteen-year-old infantryman had risked his life to save a fellow soldier who had been wounded and pinned down by enemy fire. Dodging a hail of bullets, he'd picked up the soldier, thrown him over his shoulder, and—even though wounded himself— carried him to safety. In the process, he earned his first of three Purple Hearts.

My hands trembled. They were touching the picture of a hero. A war hero. The very thought thrilled me. That this hero was my dad thrilled me even more. A newspaper had written up his story, taken his picture, and spread the news to every doorstep of Anderson, Indiana. My dad was a decorated soldier who had braved the jungles of Guadalcanal, dodging enemy fire. He had fought his way through the battlefield to reach a wounded buddy. And I knew—I knew that someday he would fight his way back and reach me. No matter what minefields he had to cross. No matter how many bullets he had to dodge.

That picture was the only one of him I had ever seen. And although my hands returned it, my heart held on to it. Every now and then, I crept back to my mother's room, to that drawer, those papers, just to make sure the picture was still there—and to kindle the hope that someday he would step out of that picture and into my life.

I held on to that hope through the end of elementary school. Through the end of junior high and throughout high school. By that time, my brothers and I were up to our shoulder pads in sports. Football, baseball, wrestling. I weighed only 160 pounds, but I made the all-city team as a linebacker, made the all-district team as a wrestler, and started as a catcher on the baseball team with my twin brother, Jeff, who was the pitcher. I was small, but I was a fighter. Just like my dad.

While Mom went to our practices, washed grass stains out of our uniforms, and cheered in the stands, I waited for Dad to fight his way home. Every game I waited. Every sport. Every father-son banquet where we had to go with a friend's father.

By now I not only missed not having a father but was also embarrassed about it. Embarrassed when I'd see a father come down from the stands at the end of a game, looking for his son to congratulate or console him. Seeing him put his arms around his son, patting him on the shoulder pads, walking with him off the field. It was all so embarrassing and painful. It stirred such a longing. Knowing that that dad was taking his boy to the drive-in for a burger and afterward would take him home. To a place where he lived with him too.

How I longed for that, ached for that, waited for that.

Finally, one fall day, the fall of my junior year, the waiting ended.

"Zoa, this is Joe." The phone call came out of the blue, without warning, without explanation, and without an apology for all the years he hadn't called, hadn't come by, hadn't communicated. "I live over by the stadium where the boys are playing on Friday, and I'd sure like to come and meet them. Would that be all right?"

A few days earlier, the local afternoon newspaper had run an article in the sports pages about our upcoming game. A reporter had come to our practice, bringing a photographer with him. He took a picture that had ended up on the front page of the sports section. The caption read, "Jeff and John Trent—Twin Starters for the Mighty Titans."

The picture had prompted the call. He said he wanted to watch my brother and me play and then we could all meet on the field afterward. Mom spoke with the head coach after the call and received permission for us to stay after the game instead of having to leave on the team bus.

The night before the game, I hardly slept. I knew my father had played a year of college football before he went to war. Now he was coming to watch us play, just as I'd always dreamed.

The day of the game, I hardly thought about anything else. We played Westwood High that night. Danny White, who went on to become an All-American at Arizona State and from there the starting quarterback for the Dallas Cowboys, led their team in a game that seesawed back and forth for three quarters. But in the final quarter, Danny's legendary arm threw two touchdown passes. We went down in defeat. But we went down fighting.

Neither Jeff nor I was discouraged about the loss. We'd played our hearts out. Not for us, not for our team, not for our coach or our school. We played our hearts out that night for our dad.

Our school, Arcadia High School, had white helmets. Westwood had orange. At that time, there was little focus on protecting players from helmet-to-helmet collisions. I'd taken off my helmet after the game. I couldn't wait to show my father all the orange paint on my helmet—my "medals" that showed I hadn't been afraid to hit someone hard. We wanted him to see the sons he hadn't seen for all these years. And when he saw us, we wanted him to be proud of us.

After the game, my mother and older brother came down from the stands to meet us. Together we walked to the place where Dad had said he would meet us. It was a moment we had waited for all our lives.

We kept our helmets off, hoping he would see us and somehow recognize us. While the fans streamed from the stands and onto the field, we searched for the hero who had finally fought his way home. As the streams thinned, our anticipation swelled.

I felt a mingling of anticipation and awkwardness, similar to what the grown-up son feels in the final scene of *Field of Dreams*, where he sees his father after many years of separation. Remember the mingling of emotions?

"Look at him," Ray Kinsella says to his wife. "He's got his whole life in front of him, and I'm not even a glint in his eye. What do I say to him?"

What *do* you say at a moment like that? To a father you have never seen, never met, never talked to? Do you run to him, walk to him, wait for him to walk to you? Do you shake hands or hug, laugh or cry, talk about the game or the war? What?

While I was wondering such things, the bus left, and the parking lot emptied. The bleachers were bare now, row after row of them staring down at us blankly, mockingly. Still we waited. Finally, someone shut off the stadium lights, leaving the four of us standing on the field.

On that dark, empty field.

He didn't show.

He was my father and a hero . . . and he didn't show.

When everything seems to be going against you, remember that the airplane takes off against the wind, not with it.

HENRY FORD

CHAPTER 11

OUT OF CONTROL

That night as the lights went out on the football field, the lights went out on my dreams. Until then, I'd had a simmering anger over his having left us. But that night it turned into a volcano. He had called. Even talked to my mother. Told us he would be there. He had not just gotten our hopes up. He had dashed years of dreams. He got us thinking that maybe we mattered. That maybe he cared. And then he didn't show.

Although my father had abandoned me—abandoned all of us—seventeen years earlier, I had never felt the pain of the abandonment in the way I did that night. And it came close to ruining me.

The ride home was quiet. We were all dealing with our feelings in our own way. As close as Jeff and I were, we didn't talk about that night, how we felt, or how we hurt. Years later, when we were in college and older, we did. But not that night. And not any night of the two remaining years we spent at home.

By the time we got home, I could have ripped the front door

off its hinges. *How could he? How could he leave us there, standing by ourselves, making fools of ourselves?*

Everyone on the team knew why we weren't going back on the bus that night. The coach knew, the players, the managers, everyone. What was I going to tell them Monday morning when they asked how it went with my dad? What was it like seeing him after all these years, and was he coming home, moving in?

I cursed his name and cursed God for passing it on to me. Son of a Trent. *You can have your name. Go ahead, take it; you've taken everything else.* I called him every rotten name I knew, and I knew plenty. All that night I wrestled with the bedsheets. I could have punched his face in; I was that mad. But I only had a pillow.

The family my father had left behind was struggling to be a family the best we could, struggling to make ends meet, to work things out, to take whatever life sent our way and make the best of it. We struggled, in a word, to survive.

Our way of surviving was not to talk about the negatives, only the positives. What we didn't talk about with one another we were left to ourselves to figure out. That's how a lot of families survive. It was the way Frederick Buechner's family survived the suicide of his father. In his autobiographical book, *Telling Secrets*, Buechner tells the story:

> There was no funeral to mark his death and put a period at the end of the sentence that had been his life, and as far as I can remember, once he had died my mother, brother, and I rarely talked about him much ever again, either to each other or to anybody else. It made my mother too sad to talk about him, and since there was already more than enough sadness to go round, my brother and I avoided the subject with her as she avoided it for her own reasons also with us. . . .
>
> We didn't talk about my father with each other, and we didn't talk about him outside the family either partly

at least because suicide was looked on as something a little shabby and shameful in those days. Nice people weren't supposed to get mixed up with it. . . . His suicide was a secret we nonetheless tried to keep as best we could, and after a while my father himself became such a secret. . . .

Within a year of his death I seem to have forgotten what he looked like except for certain photographs of him, to have forgotten what his voice sounded like and what it had been like to be with him. Because none of the three of us ever talked about how we had felt about him when he was alive or how we felt about him now that he wasn't, those feelings soon disappeared too and went underground along with the memories.[1]

The memory of that dark Friday night on that empty football field went underground too. But it didn't stay there. Neither did the feelings.

The feelings I had before that night were mostly positive. Mom had given us a lot of love, a lot of good memories. Some of my fondest were the times Mom would take us to the library, where she looked for books to help her with the battles she was forced to fight. The battle of a woman in the 1950s and '60s, fighting for a career. The battle of a single parent raising a houseful of boys. And the battle against rheumatoid arthritis, which was crippling her.

When she looked for her books at the library, she let us roam around looking for ours. Where I looked most often was the section on World War II. Unconsciously, I was building a bridge to the past, hoping I might meet my father somewhere back there. Maybe in a picture of Guadalcanal. Maybe in a story. I wanted so much to connect with him, and the library seemed like the only place that even dimly remembered where he might be.

One of the other subliminal influences my father's war picture had on me was that it made me want to wear a uniform like his.

But a boy can play soldier only so long. After that, what battles does a growing boy fight, what uniforms does he wear?

A football uniform was the one I wore, and a hundred yards of stadium grass were my battlefield. Though my father wasn't at the games where I played or at the banquets where I was applauded, I always felt that the press clippings and awards would one day make him proud of me. Maybe it was another bridge I was trying to build. And maybe those were the only materials I had to build it.

All I know is that when he didn't show, the bridge collapsed.

The hurt I felt that night turned almost instantaneously to anger, which I bottled as bitterness. I was like a shaken soda bottle, waiting for someone, daring someone, to pry off the cap. When that happened, everything I kept bottled up inside spewed out. Where it happened most often was on the football field.

I was like a shaken soda bottle, waiting for someone, daring someone, to pry off the cap.

I threw myself into each game with abandon. I hit hard, recklessly, and without concern for those around me. I felt the rush of the hunt and the thrill of first blood, but I felt nothing for those I left in my wake.

Activity was the drug I used to keep from feeling. I kept on the run, never allowing myself time to think about anything, feel anything. I revved up the RPMs on our '64 green VW bug and kept them revved until I coasted into the driveway late at night and fell into bed exhausted. The amphetamine of activity that masked my pain also masked the pain I was causing to other people. I had no awareness of those around me, no understanding for them, no compassion, certainly no love or forgiveness.

I can see that now, looking back, especially when I consider my relationships with girls. The relationships were all short-lived because as soon as a girl started getting serious, I dropped her. Except I would never tell her I'd dropped her. Instead of meeting her after her class to walk her to the next one, I just didn't show. I took another stairway, went down another hallway, simply avoiding her. I never said a word, sent a note, or made a phone call. In a few days or so, I figured she would have gotten the message. It was all so easy. I simply walked another way to class. That way I didn't have to process anything, say anything, feel anything, be responsible for anything—really care about or connect with anyone.

While I was so smoothly sidestepping the deeper issues in my life, my mom was having trouble just walking. The pain of her arthritis had grown debilitating, and she desperately needed another surgery. Her uncle was a surgeon in Indiana, and since the surgery was so expensive and the therapy so extensive, she moved there for the remainder of the year, just as she had when I was eleven. This time her sister, Aunt Dovie, moved in.

For six months she looked after us, or tried to. And for six months I took it upon myself to be the one to ruffle Aunt Dovie's feathers. I treated her like dirt. I snuck out almost every night, telling her off whenever she confronted me about it.

By now I was fluent in cursing. It may not seem like such a big deal today for a teenager to curse, but back then, if a coach heard you so much as whisper a swear word, you took a lap for it. Besides taking more laps that year, I lapped up more beer, getting drunk at parties and afterward getting into trouble. Some of the trouble I got into involved stealing. I didn't steal because I wanted things, not material things anyway. I stole because I wanted something else. Acceptance, or maybe a family. Maybe that's why being in a gang appealed to me.

They called themselves the Leaches, and to get in I had to steal a dozen gearshift knobs from cars. Done. What next? Stereo? No sweat. The stereo we took was from an abandoned house, so we didn't think it was a big deal. The police thought differently. Aunt Dovie tried to talk with me, help me the best she could, but I just stared a hole through her, spitting in defiance at the ground where she stood.

My callousness turned to harshness. At school one day, I beat up a kid just for looking at me in a way I felt was disrespectful. After school I was worse, especially when I was with my drinking buddies. One night seven of us beat up a carful of boys from another school, smashed their car windows, and sped off laughing. I pushed aside any thought of that night.

The boys we beat up, however, didn't. When the police investigated the incident, I was pulled out of class for questioning. I didn't confess what I had done, didn't rat on my friends. And I didn't feel anything for the guys we had harmed. But for the first time in a long time, I felt something. It wasn't guilt, wasn't shame, wasn't remorse. It was embarrassment.

They had taken me out of class in front of a number of my friends.

My life was out of control.

Aunt Dovie knew it.

I knew it.

Now the whole school knew it.

Your present circumstances don't determine where you can go; they merely determine where you start.

NIDO QUBEIN, *How to Be a Great Communicator: In Person, on Paper, and on the Podium*

CHAPTER 12

THE MOMENT
JESUS BROKE IN

The picture I was left with on the football field the night my father never showed up was more painful than all the ones his absence had left for the previous seventeen years. It was a picture I tried to tear up and throw out. But no matter how I tried, I couldn't get rid of it. It lived in me, seethed in me. I was angry—so very, very angry.

Anger, says Gerald Sittser in his book *A Grace Disguised*, "is simply another way of deflecting the pain, holding it off, fighting back at it. . . . But the pain of loss is unrelenting. It stalks and chases until it catches us. It is as persistent as wind on the prairies, as constant as cold in the Antarctic, as erosive as a spring flood."[1]

The pain of losing my father was compounded by the fact that I'd been so close to getting him back. So close to filling in all those missing years, all those missing memories, all those Christmases and birthdays and ball games.

When he didn't show up that night, the pain was so unrelenting that I ran from it. But the pain stalked me. Now no matter how fast or how far I ran, it always caught up with me. When it did, the only thing I had to defend myself with was anger. So I held my anger close. And although it was sheathed at my side, my hand was always on its hilt, ready to strike. I held on to that anger throughout my junior year . . .

Until Doug Barram disarmed me.

His stature alone was disarming. He stood six foot four and weighed probably 225 pounds. He was right out of college and still in great shape from the years he'd played offensive tackle at Chico State. Doug was the Young Life leader who had come to start a new club at our high school. He was also the warmest, gentlest, most loving man I'd ever met. He had an ever-present smile, bright blue eyes that were always glad to see me, a genuine enthusiasm in his voice, and huge arms that smothered me when he hugged me.

I first met Doug when I was a freshman. He would show up after school to watch the freshman squad practice. A few members of the players' immediate families came to the games, but hardly anyone came to the practices. Doug was one of the conspicuous few. He stood on the sidelines, watching us, encouraging us, patting us on the shoulder pads and, as Young Life leaders are so wonderful at doing, earning the right to be heard.

One picture particularly stands out in my memories of him. We had just lost a real heartbreaker of a game. I kept my helmet on because I was crying and didn't want anybody to see. Then, running onto the field, this bear of a man came up to me, tears streaming down his face, and hugged me. It was Doug. I'd never seen a grown man cry before, especially not a man like him, so big and an athlete.

I saw Doug on the sidelines of my life a lot over my high school years. I still remember the way he looked at me. The delight in his eyes whenever he'd see me on the field, in the gym, at school. I still remember the excitement in his voice whenever he talked with me on the sidelines before the game or on the field after it. And it wasn't just me. I saw Doug befriend all sorts of people, people

I wouldn't have wasted my breath saying hi to in the halls. But he said hi. And he had the same excitement in his voice when he said it to them as when he said it to me, had the same delight in his eyes, the same kindness, the same interest, the same genuineness.

From my freshman year through my sophomore year and on into my junior year, Doug Barram left a lot of pictures in my life. He spent time with a number of us at the high school, talking about things that were important to us, laughing at things we thought were funny. There was always an open invitation at his house for any of us who wanted a place to hang.

For hours in his backyard, we'd play "bull moose" football, a slow-motion game of tackle football that could be amazingly violent. Then we'd stop, and his wife would bring out Cokes, and we'd have Campaigners. That was a Bible study I'd put up with for the chance to be around a family like his.

Sometimes we'd get invited to dinner. His family would talk and laugh, ask questions of each other. I saw him kiss his wife and tell her he loved her. And I knew it was true. I saw it in his eyes and saw it reflected in hers. I heard it in the tone of his voice as he said everything from "Pass the butter" to "Tell me about your day."

I knew his words were real because his pictures were real.

At dinner, before you ate at the Barram house, you had to hold hands with whomever was next to you. And you'd pray for the food. I had prayed before, but it was always things like *God, if You get me out of this, I promise I'll never do anything wrong again!* But I'd never really prayed. Not like Doug. I'd listen as it seemed like he was really talking to someone. My prayers were to win a game or get out of trouble, and they sounded so hollow, so artificial, next to his.

I knew his words were real because his pictures were real. All those pictures I had of him standing on the sidelines. Pictures of him bundling up his kids at night, of him kissing them, wrestling with them, answering their questions, telling them stories, praying with them. Blessing them. The first time I saw a father blessing a son wasn't in Scripture. It was Doug holding Mike and then Andy and praying a blessing over them in the hallway. And I knew he meant every word, every hug, every prayer, every blessing.

Whatever it was he had, I knew it was real. And I knew it was something I needed so much. Wanted so much. It was who I wanted to be as a man, as a husband one day, as a father. I wanted to be around it so much that every week or so I would drive to his house and mow his yard, just for an excuse to be there, just to see it all, just to experience what all of them had.

A family with a father. A father who showed up. A father who was there and who *loved* being there. And a father who had a real faith in something I'd totally dismissed but that was beginning to break through even my shell of anger.

As I pulled the mower out of my Volkswagen van and started mowing his yard, Doug would come outside, drawn by the noise. He always offered to pay me for mowing the yard, knowing how tight things were in our home. I always turned it down. But then he'd say, "Well . . . how about coming in for dinner when you get done?" Which I "reluctantly" accepted, thinking again that I had tricked him into inviting me into his home when he knew what I was doing all along.

The pictures were so compelling. I only mowed his yard, but I would have painted his house, shingled his roof, cleaned out his garage—anything. I'd do anything just to be there and be a part of it, even if the part was just a yard boy looking in at it all from the outside.

During my junior year, when all that anger was working itself through my life, Doug invited Jeff and me, along with four other football players, to a movie. It was in a regular theater I'd been to plenty of times, the Kachina Theatre on Scottsdale Road.

We had no idea it was a religious film. He didn't tell us *that*.

To be honest, the film was terrible, the worst I had ever seen, or so I thought at the time. And by the time it was over, I was beyond antsy to get out of there. But when the houselights came on, there was a man standing in front of the theater, getting ready to speak into a microphone.

My heart sank because I knew I wouldn't be getting out of there anytime soon. The man gave a short testimonial, and then he said something that shook me.

"Is anyone here ready to change the pictures of your life story?"

That opened my ears and made me sit up.

"You can tonight, by inviting Jesus into your heart."

And he gave us the opportunity to come forward and place our faith in Christ.

I thought as I sat there, *I still have my senior year ahead of me. The parties. The good times. The cruisin' and boozin'. Nope. Won't be me breaking ranks.* I wedged myself a little more snugly into my velvet cushioned seat. And from that seat, I looked down the row at Jeff. Then at my friends from the football team. And finally at Doug.

Suddenly, unexpectedly, there was one of those *moments* we've written about many times already. Like Helen had in reading a book. Like I had the Christmas years before without any presents and still didn't fully understand. I understood now.

There was a moment when, all of a sudden, I realized that as I looked down the row, I was looking at a six-foot-four Jesus. It was He who was calling me that night. He who was offering life. He who was offering forgiveness from all the anger. Healing from all the shame I was carrying. He who stood there with open arms, ready to bless me. To tell me He loved me. "Come on down, Son."

I stood up. Jeff stood up. All but one of my friends stood up too. Hayes and Chuck and Don. All five of us filed out of our row and into the aisle, then down to the front, where that man stood. Doug stood to the side as well.

All five of us came to know Jesus that night. Doug prayed with each of us. (And even today we're all still friends and still loving

Jesus, except for Don, who died in a plane crash and beat all of us home to heaven.)

Something moved me that night at the theater. What was it? What was it that touched my heart and turned my life around? It wasn't the film. It wasn't the appeal of the man at the front of the theater. What, then?

I think it was the cumulative effect of all the pictures Doug Barram had left in my life. At that moment, the Holy Spirit brought those pictures together to form a composite. When I leaned forward in our aisle and saw Doug, the picture I saw was Jesus. It was Jesus I had heard in Doug's voice. Jesus I had seen in his smile. Jesus I had felt in his hugs, in his home, in his heart. All along, it was Jesus he was showing me.

I knew that if I were ever going to have a home like Doug's, a marriage like his, a family like his, a life like his, I had to have in my heart what he had in his.

I didn't know a lot about this Jesus. But I knew that if I were ever going to have a home like Doug's, a marriage like his, a family like his, a life like his, I had to have in my heart what he had in his. I had to have Jesus.

No, it wasn't the film that moved me that night.

It wasn't the man at the front of the theater.

It was a picture. A composite of all the pictures of blessing that Doug Barram had left in my life. That night they moved me. Out of my seat. Onto my knees. And into the Kingdom of God.

We have no control over the stories into which we are born and little over those in which we are raised. They are as much an inheritance as our genetic code, creating roles for us to play as surely as our DNA maps a future for our bodies. . . . We can change our stories only by changing our choices.

DANIEL TAYLOR, *The Healing Power of Stories: Creating Yourself through the Stories of Your Life*

CHAPTER 13

CHOOSING TO CHANGE

I wasn't sure what all happened at the movie theater that night. But I knew what I had to do when I got home. Before we all left, Doug had handed each of us a gift and a homework assignment.

The gift was a Bible, the first Bible I had ever owned. And the homework assignment was to read a verse he had underlined for each of us. For me, the verse was Hebrews 13:5. Doug looked me in the eyes and said, "Go home and read this verse *a hundred times.*"

It had been such an amazing night. I wasn't ready to go to bed when I got home. So I sat down in my room to do my first-ever Bible homework. Only later did I find out that Doug wasn't being literal. He was being metaphorical, as in *"Go home and read this a lot."*

What I heard, though—I think by the Spirit of God—were his *literal* words: *"Go home and read this verse a hundred times."*

So that's what I set out to do that night. And it changed my life.

The verse reads, speaking of Jesus, "For He Himself has said, 'I WILL NEVER DESERT YOU, NOR WILL I EVER ABANDON YOU.'"

I took out a sheet of paper and a pen. I read the verse for the first time. And I made a tally mark. Then I read it a second time.

"For He Himself has said, 'I WILL NEVER DESERT YOU, NOR WILL I EVER ABANDON YOU.'"

Then I put a second tally mark on the paper. And yes, when I got to five, I made a diagonal line. On I went. Four marks and a diagonal line. Reading that verse over and over. Making those marks. Five, ten, fifteen, twenty times. But I never got to one hundred.

Here again is an example of a moment when God broke into a life story. I had gotten to the sixties when I realized it wasn't just me reading the verse. *That verse was reading me.* Not only that, but I was also weeping. Bawling. I hadn't cried like that for years.

It was as if Jesus were sitting right there with me, patiently waiting for me to read that verse one hundred times. Wanting to make sure I got the picture, just as Doug had waited patiently for years for me to accept Jesus. It was as if I needed to know right then, from that moment to every day after, that those words were literally true.

My father had chosen to leave. My mother had been forced to leave for her surgeries. But I had someone in my life who would never, ever desert me or abandon me. And because of that, I realized I didn't have to do life alone anymore. That no one does who is in Christ. I had His blessing. I could change. *I had changed.*

Can You Really Know Things Can Change?

That evening was a Saturday. (I still have the ticket stub from that crummy movie and wonderful night.) I had the best night's sleep I could remember. But the next morning, I wasn't sure about all that had happened at the theater or in reading that verse so many times. Still, even though I couldn't explain it all, I knew it was real. What I didn't know was how much difference it would begin to make in my life.

Until the following Monday.

I was in PE class, assigned by the teacher to play tennis with this small, dorky guy who was running me ragged and beating me like a drum. Normally I would have done something stupid like yell, curse, throw my racket into the net, grit my teeth, and give him a stare that would melt a glacier. But here I was getting strummed by someone, and I didn't do any of those things.

By the middle of the match, a sudden awareness swept over me. *I wasn't angry.*

Not at him. Not at myself. Not at my racket. Not at anything. I couldn't believe it. I was getting beaten—humiliated—and I wasn't getting angry.

Only the week before, I had been thrown out of a football game for my anger. I could never predict when it would erupt, much less control the eruption. My anger seemed to be always running just beneath the surface, like magma beneath the earth's crust, coursing to find some opening so it could vent itself. And it didn't need much of an opening. A sarcastic remark on the football field. A smirky look in the hall. A lopsided score on the tennis court.

But now, there I was on the tennis court, on the losing side of the score, a small, dorky guy on the other side of the net acing me . . . and I wasn't angry. I went to school in Arizona. It was hot outside. But I stood there, and chills swept over me on a ninety-degree day.

That was the first thing that happened that helped me see that Jesus was real and in my life—and able to help me change my life story.

If anybody needed it to be real, needed to know the genuine commitment that Jesus promised, it was me. I'm convinced that the character qualities of the peer group I was hanging with—and the anger, the inability to forgive, the harshness and callousness—would have one day turned into dark alleys, drugs, or self-medicating addiction like my father. Who knows?

What I do know is this: Even though I hadn't read this passage in the Bible yet, when I did read it, I knew it was describing me:

> You were dead in your offenses and sins, in which you previously walked . . . and were by nature children of wrath. . . . But God, being rich in mercy, because of His great love with which He loved us, even when we were dead in our wrongdoings, made us alive together with Christ (by grace you have been saved).
>
> EPHESIANS 2:1, 3-5

I knew two things after that weekend. First, that Jesus would never leave me or forsake me. Attachment bond of all attachment bonds. And I knew that because of His presence, commitment, and blessing, *I could change.* In Christ, I didn't have to let all my anger and loneliness own me. By grace I had been saved. And then, the very next day, I needed the reminder that life could be different.

The next day, my dad called the house again. Out of the blue like his first call, this time he called to apologize about missing the game and ask for another time to get together. He picked a neutral site, a Chinese restaurant. It was a safe place to meet—safe from anybody's emotions spewing out, safe from confrontation, safe from the possibilities of the evening running long.

In Christ, I didn't have to let all that anger and loneliness own me.

I'll spare the details so as not to be dishonoring, saying only that the best parts of the evening were awkward. The worst, because of the alcohol, were sad and embarrassing. And by the time we had gotten to our fortune cookies, I had lost my appetite for the relationship that all my life I had hungered to have. I had thought that meeting my father was the most important thing I needed to change and be whole. But that night, I sat there knowing it was my heavenly Father's blessing that had saved me. Rescued me. The Lord's blessing was what I needed most.

Dad had remarried, we were told. Had two kids, we were told. And for the past seventeen years, he had lived within twenty miles of where we lived. Twenty miles from where we lived out our childhood. Twenty miles from where we'd played soldiers on Camelback Mountain, living on the hand-me-down hope that the hero would one day come home.

Twenty miles. And never a visit, never a call, never a card. Nothing.

After that night, he tried a time or two to step back into our lives with years between each call, but the steps were halting and didn't cover much distance. He invited us to his house, where we met his wife and kids—a boy and a girl who were wonderful, who would have been great to get to know.

He and I didn't have a lot of common ground except for his involvement in the war and my interest in it. So that's what we talked about. Vietnam was raging on the other side of the world, on college campuses across the nation, and on the nightly news. As a kid who had grown up watching John Wayne fight his way through the Pacific and who had stormed my own way over hill and dale of Camelback Mountain, the idea of going off to war seemed a romantic notion. Maybe after my senior year I would enlist.

The stories my dad told that night at the restaurant were intoxicating. He talked about how they used to catch fish by throwing percussion grenades into the water. When the grenade went off, the fish floated belly-up to the surface. Then Dad and his buddies cooked them in banana leaves. Stories like that.

But then the stories turned sober. He told about being under mortar attack and taking a direct hit to his foxhole that tore off his backpack and shredded his clothes. He barely escaped with his life. He told about replacements coming from the ship and how if they snored for two nights in a row, they were "put on point," sent to lookout posts on the perimeter. Many of them never came back. You see, snoring lets the enemy know where you're hiding.

"You don't snore, do you?" he asked. I said no, but the truth is, I didn't know. What if I did? And what if I got drafted? What if I snored two nights in a row and got put on point? Suddenly the reality of war fell into my thoughts like a mortar, shredding all my romantic notions.

The stories continued into the evening. Stories of how the Japanese would booby-trap jewelry boxes, map cases—anything that might appeal to an American soldier enough for him to pick it up for a closer look. He told us about a time when he was out on patrol and some of his buddies came across a trove of trinkets. Before my dad could get there to stop them, the booby trap went off, killing two and mangling the rest.

Then he told the story of a time he was on his way to officer training camp. He was on a troop train with almost a hundred college men, all slated to go to officer candidate school. But someone had brought a crate of liquor, and almost all the men, including my father, had gotten falling-down drunk.

When the train pulled into the depot, the camp commandant was so infuriated by what he saw that he ordered everyone back on the train. They were no longer coming to camp to be officers. He sent the train on to boot camp, where they would all be privates. Forget officers' school or any stateside staff jobs. Everyone on that train, he said, went through infantry school, and they were some of the first to go into combat in the Pacific. And three-fourths of those men were killed.

As I listened, I wondered, *Are these the stories I'll be telling years from now? And will I someday become the man who's telling them now?*

If that's the path my father took, would that be mine?

He was my biological father. From the picture I had of him, I always assumed I would become like him. He had given me life and half my genetic code. That code had determined my height and the color of my hair. What other things had it determined? Had it determined what kind of man I would become, what kind of father? Or did I have some say in the matter, some control over the story?

In his book *The Healing Power of Stories*, Daniel Taylor addresses those questions:

> Stories link past, present, and future in a way that tells us where we have been (even before we were born), where we are, and where we could be going.
>
> Our stories teach us that there is a place for us, that we fit. They suggest to us that our lives can have a plot. Stories turn mere chronology, one thing after another, into the purposeful action of plot, and thereby into meaning.
>
> If we discern a plot to our lives, we are more likely to take ourselves and our lives seriously. If nothing is connected, then nothing matters. Stories are the single best way humans have for accounting for our experience. They help us see how choices and events are tied together, why things are and how things could be.
>
> Healthy stories challenge us to be active characters, not passive victims or observers. Both the present and the future are determined by choices, and choice is the essence of character. If we see ourselves as active characters in our own stories, we can exercise our human freedom to choose a present and future for ourselves and for those we love that gives life meaning.[1]

Somewhere in my subconscious, as I spoke with my father, all those pictures of my life up to then came back. Pictures of my childhood. All those times when I'd felt the loss of a father. Then finally meeting him. And all that had happened in coming to know Jesus. And I realized the pictures I held of Doug, my spiritual father, were very different from those I had of my own dad. Such opposite pictures. They told such different stories.

I didn't realize the full implications of the choice I had made that night in the movie theater, but one thing was clear: When I got out of my seat and went forward at that movie theater, I made a choice about which picture I was going to live by. Because of Jesus, I *could* change the story.

The moment the young child becomes reflective, however, is the moment the child begins developing the ability to choose rather than simply inherit a story. At the heart of reflection is the weighing of multiple possibilities—possible explanations, possible choices, possible consequences. The first suspicion that something could be different than it is signals the initial stirrings of character and the potential to choose one's story.

DANIEL TAYLOR, *The Healing Power of Stories: Creating Yourself through the Stories of Your Life*

CHAPTER 14

WHEN YOU NEED
TO SWITCH FATHERS

By laying out my story, I hope you've seen things in your life that have begun to resonate. You may have missed the Blessing like I did, perhaps in even more dramatic or difficult ways. But all our paths lead to a turning point.

To a choice.

The choice I made at seventeen, the choice you may need to make, isn't something new. We can see an amazing picture of it in the choice a young boy made centuries ago. If you've never read about him, it's an amazing story of how anyone, even someone from the worst of backgrounds, can make a change.

Josiah looked at the pictures of his life and made a choice. Not as a teenager like me but as a child. Josiah was only eight. He was one of the rulers of the southern kingdom in ancient Judah during the divided monarchy. The reign passed from father to son, generation after generation. Josiah had received it from his father, Amon, who had received it from his father, Manasseh.

In 2 Kings 21, the Scriptures describe the reign of Josiah's grandfather:

> Manasseh was twelve years old when he became king, and he reigned for fifty-five years in Jerusalem; and his mother's name was Hephzibah. He did evil in the sight of the LORD, in accordance with the abominations of the nations whom the LORD dispossessed before the sons of Israel. For he rebuilt the high places which his father Hezekiah had destroyed; and he erected altars for Baal and made an Asherah, just as Ahab king of Israel had done, and he worshiped all the heavenly lights and served them. And he built altars in the house of the LORD, of which the LORD had said, "In Jerusalem I will put My name."
> 2 KINGS 21:1-4

Then here come some of the horrific things Manasseh added to his list of evils:

> He built altars for all the heavenly lights in the two courtyards of the house of the LORD. And he made his son pass through the fire, interpreted signs, practiced divination, and used mediums and spiritists. He did great evil in the sight of the LORD, provoking Him to anger.
> 2 KINGS 21:5-6

Those altars he built were for child sacrifice. Those people he surrounded himself with were consorting with demonic powers. Manasseh's reign was characterized by widespread apostasy and wholesale wickedness, with prostitutes offering their services in the Temple and children being offered as sacrifices on those altars and just outside the city in the Valley of Hinnom. So great was the influence of Manasseh's wickedness that he pushed the entire nation into doing more evil than the Canaanites, who lived near them, people God had driven out of the land centuries earlier (2 Kings 21:9).

In life, he had set the standard for evil actions by a king of Judah. But that didn't stop with his death. When Manasseh died, he wanted to make sure that his legacy of evil stayed front and center in his home and with his family.

But how to do that when you're dead? Manasseh came up with a way. "And Manasseh lay down with his fathers and was buried in the garden of his own house, in the garden of Uzza" (2 Kings 21:18).

Every day, then, everyone in his family who lived there would need to walk past his grave. Think of the most evil Mafia kingpin you've heard about. Can you think of any of them who demanded to be buried in the middle of their own home?

We are often told, "Like father, like son. Like mother, like daughter." It's almost a certainty that history repeats itself. Manasseh certainly succeeded in passing down a legacy of evil to the next generation. For we read,

> Amon was twenty-two years old when he became king,
> and he reigned two years in Jerusalem. . . . He did evil
> in the sight of the LORD, just as his father Manasseh had
> done. For he walked entirely in the way that his father had
> walked, and served the idols that his father had served,
> and worshiped them. So he abandoned the LORD, the God
> of his fathers, and did not walk in the way of the LORD.
> 2 KINGS 21:19-22

That's just what we and the social scientists would have expected. After all, Amon had been raised in a culture of death and evil. We shouldn't be surprised that he followed his father's pattern. In fact, we're told that "he walked entirely in the way that his father had walked." That is, until a palace conspiracy cut short Amon's reign. Scripture tells us he was slaughtered in his own home by those terrible people he'd surrounded himself with!

And—like father, like son—Amon also wanted to make sure his imprint on his son would be passed down, not forgotten. So, just like his father, Amon chose to be buried right in his home. "He was buried in his grave in the garden of Uzza" (2 Kings 21:26).

Now Amon's son, a boy king, ascended the throne.

Think about the background Josiah brought with him. His grandfather was not just a king but the king of wickedness and evil. His own father, who had just been murdered, was every bit as bad.

Today, we'd call this a clear multigenerational, systemic, circular pattern—one repeated and passed down from father to son. We see it constantly, and for most it's considered settled science. Thus we'd expect that the next words in Scripture concerning Josiah would be "And Amon's son Josiah became king, and he walked in all the ways of his grandfather Manasseh and his father, Amon, and he also did evil in God's sight."

After all, why not? History is destiny, right? Yet while we absolutely do see generational transmission take place, it's of a very different kind!

The Choice Many of Us Need to Make Today

Here is what 2 Kings 21 actually goes on to say: "Josiah was eight years old when he became king. . . . He did what was right in the sight of the LORD *and walked entirely in the way of his father David*" (2 Kings 22:1-2, emphasis added).

Wait a moment. He did what? Not evil?

And what about Josiah's following a different father—David?

Is that an example of an error in the Bible? Certainly not.

Josiah's biological father was indeed Amon. But Josiah, even at eight years old, realized he had a choice. *History is not destiny when God's love and life and blessing give us the ability to change the pictures.*

Josiah chose a different generational pattern. He skipped back 350 years to pick a model for his life story, a king named David. He wanted a godly ancestor to fol-

Josiah, even at eight years old, realized he had a choice.

low and model his life after. King David wasn't perfect, but he was still a man after God's own heart. And such a man would Josiah become as well.

* * *

I've spoken with many people whose story of missing the Blessing involved far more pain and difficulty than mine. But I haven't spoken to anyone whose background was any worse than Josiah's. His grandfather slaughtered infants and led a whole nation into evil, and his father was just as evil until he was murdered in his own home.

Josiah inherited not only the throne but also a dark and distorted picture of what the person looked like who sat on that throne. But like us, Josiah had a choice: He could live by the pictures he was left with or he could look through the family album for some other picture to live by.

He needed to go back a number of generations, stopping at the picture of David, Israel's greatest king. David was very human, his life filled with turmoil and tragedy. He failed in many ways. But he owned up to his failures and humbled himself and sought forgiveness. He was a man with feet of clay, but at his very core, he was a man after God's own heart (see Acts 13:22).

Looking at the pictures, Josiah decided to step away from his physical father and into line with an ancestor from a decidedly stronger spiritual lineage. In doing so, he changed the story of his life. When he made that choice, he was able to reverse the curse that had been handed him and live out the Blessing. That choice changed not only his future, but also the future of Judah.

> The three decades of Josiah's reign were among the happiest in Judah's experience. They were characterized by peace, prosperity, and reform. No outside enemies made war, the people could concentrate on constructive activity, and Josiah himself sought to please God by reinstituting matters commanded in the Mosaic Law.[1]

The choice Josiah made can't be mandated by committee, whether that committee is the Supreme Court or the local church. You don't walk away from a background like his by having more education or indoctrination or legislation.

What changed is the same thing that can reverse the curse we've been surrounded with—that God-given grace and power to make a different choice. We can choose to change our story by changing the pictures that influence it.

What's so remarkable about the power of that choice is that it doesn't just stop the flow of negative pictures handed down from one generation to the next. It actually *reverses* the flow. We can choose which pictures we live by, and we can choose which pictures we leave behind. We can move from death to life, from curse to blessing, the same way Josiah did.

A record of some of those pictures is found in 2 Kings 23. So remarkable was Josiah's influence that the Scriptures memorialized him with this tribute: "Before him there was no king like him who turned to the LORD with all his heart, all his soul, and all his might, in conformity to all the law of Moses; nor did any like him arise after him" (2 Kings 23:25).

Not a bad caption for the pictures he left behind.

I'd settle for it in a heartbeat.

Thankfully, according to God's Word, we all can.

In another dramatic Old Testament story, God shares an amazing truth with His people, a truth Josiah would have read about in his public reading of the Law.

Under the inspired leadership of Moses, the nation of Israel had emerged from hundreds of years of slavery and crossed an inhospitable desert. But even then, their misery was compounded. For along the way, they received neither food nor water from the hands of those already living in the land. One king in particular even hired a noted sorcerer, Balaam, to curse them.

We can pick new pictures of blessing, even if we never saw them growing up.

But listen to God's words to His own people in response to what they suffered: "The LORD your God was unwilling to listen to Balaam, but the LORD your God turned the curse into a blessing for you because the LORD your God loves you" (Deuteronomy 23:5).

His love reverses the curse.

His love replaces the curse with the Blessing.

Did you notice how "the LORD your God" is repeated three times? It's hard to miss that picture. Hard to miss the fact that, as Josiah did, as I had to do, and *as you may have to do*, we can choose pictures other than the ones we were given. We can pick new pictures of blessing, even if we never saw them growing up.

Can You Switch Fathers without Hate or Dishonor?

I'll close this picture of the journey I had to take from missing to receiving the Blessing by making sure one thing is clear. The first of the Ten Commandments with a promise reads, "Honor your father and your mother, so that your days may be prolonged on the land which the LORD your God gives you" (Exodus 20:12).

On that day and on the many since I "switched fathers," it wasn't an act of dishonor or a "getting back at him" backlash. *After I came to Christ*, I did try to build a relationship with my dad for the rest of his life. I was there at the end of his life when he went from one hospital and hospice to another. I held his hand for eight hours on the day he died as he struggled to breathe with congestive heart failure. I was there when he breathed his last. It was 4:43 on that August afternoon when he died, and he had still never spoken words of blessing.

I wish I could conclude my story with the kind of Hollywood ending where everything wraps up wonderfully in the final scene—something like in *Field of Dreams*, where father and son do miraculously meet and repair their relationship.

But for me, that's not what happened. There would never be a blessing from him to me or my brothers. In Christ, however, I could still honor my father but choose not to repeat the choices and pictures he'd left. I could pick a different father to model my life after.

You can as well.

• • •

That's my (John's) story, from childhood hurt to God's breaking in. You've seen the pictures from my journey—missing my own father's blessing, then receiving the Blessing from my spiritual father and my Lord. Now let's take a look at Kari's story, where her pictures became terrible and unbearable. Yet even in that darkness, light and blessing broke through. Indeed, ultimately, the only thing strong enough to overcome the curse is God's blessing, which can change everything.

After Kari's story, we'll keep on with your journey, looking at the small steps Kari and I took to move toward blessing.

But as for me, I will sing of Your strength;
Yes, I will joyfully sing of Your faithfulness in the morning,
For You have been my refuge
And a place of refuge on the day of my distress.

PSALM 59:16

CHAPTER 15

THERE CAN BE LIGHT
IN THE DARKEST PLACE

I (Kari) was blessed to grow up in a home that shone with light, love, the Blessing, and Jesus. Yet I, too, have a story of brokenness. And even more important, I have an amazing story of God's redemption.

While the Blessing was freely given and truly lived out in my home, at the end of the day, choosing to *receive* it is every bit as necessary as choosing to *give* it.

Kari's Story

My parents blessed me regularly, yet I struggled to receive the truth from them. You see, the people I was around *outside* my home didn't seem to share the same view about my worth or my value. My house was vandalized with spray paint that said words I won't repeat here. I wasn't asked to prom, homecoming, or any significant coed social event. Rumors were spread about me. One rumor even required my dad to go to the principal's office and tell her and my teachers clearly and directly that he was not writing my school papers for me. To say the least, I wasn't exactly hearing that I had the value my parents claimed they saw in me at home.

Even more, God felt incredibly abstract to me, like an untouchable, unrelatable, uninvolved, ever-present shadow that demanded obedience to outdated rules and ideas while not providing any tangible or visible benefits. I always believed Jesus was real and even the Savior. But what was the point of following someone who didn't seem to care about me?

After I graduated from high school, I made the decision to run from those I went to school with and from God. I headed from Arizona to California and to what I hoped was a fresh start.

But all too soon, my ability to see and believe the truths I had been raised with were challenged in even greater ways. I began to try the world's ways to find joy, purpose, and identity, but I found myself becoming increasingly more depressed and hopeless. Add in an incident with sexual assault and later a boyfriend who told me he was embarrassed by me and our relationship "because you aren't perfect"—soon I was a complete and utter mess.

Enter my knight in shining armor. Or so I thought.

When I met Adam (not his real name), I finally felt seen. I finally felt valued. I felt as if someone besides my parents saw incredible things in me and actually wanted to be with me. It was like being placed on a pedestal where I was valued, admired, and desired. It was everything I had been looking for. Until it wasn't.

Slowly, things began to change. Value looked more like "You don't measure up." Admiration turned into "Change everything about yourself." And desire turned into control. Eventually, each of these became full-on abuse. Verbal. Emotional. Spiritual. Sexual. And finally, physical.

This was decades before the #MeToo movement, and I had never known of anyone who had been through abuse before. Not only was I unaware of the warning signs, but I didn't even think it was possible for something like abuse to happen to me. Yet it was happening. And I'm thankful that even when I wasn't walking with Him, God brought people into my life who saw the truth of what was occurring and had the courage to speak out on my behalf.

Neighbors called the police. One gave me a key to her apartment "in case you need a safe place to stay." Friends told me something was very wrong in my relationship. A family member gave me a book on verbal abuse, and it opened my eyes to the reality of what was happening in my relationship.

I was desperate for him to see me the way he had at the beginning of our relationship.

The problem was that this man and this relationship had become my identity. And I was determined to be good enough. I was desperate for him to see me the way he had at the beginning of our relationship—to experience those feelings of value, admiration, and desire again. I had built my entire identity on it.

So I stayed. I stayed when he kicked me out of his car and left me on the side of the freeway without my purse or cell phone.

I stayed when he called me names that cut me to pieces and led me to believe I was as worthless as I'd always assumed.

I stayed when he lied about cheating.

I stayed when he choked me. Threw things at me. Pinned me down. And threw me into a door.

I stayed when he would smile casually and tell me, "I could kill you and bury you in the desert, and no one would ever find you."

I stayed.

As anyone who has been through abuse knows, there are a million reasons I stayed. The cycle of abuse itself (abusive incident followed by the makeup/honeymoon phase, in which the abuser promises to change and once again becomes the kind and loving person he used to be, followed by the building phase, where tension is mounting, followed by another incident) was one reason.

Its very nature keeps both victim and abuser cycling through this destructive pattern. But the reality was that I also didn't believe I had any value outside this man. I was terrified—of him and of what would happen if I left. Plus I desperately wanted him to change, and I chose to believe promise after promise that he would "this time" because I loved him—or at least the *him* I had met at the beginning of our relationship.

And if I'm being totally honest, I desperately wanted to be enough. Enough to make him change. To finally know once and for all that my worth and value were real and secure. After all, he wouldn't treat me that way if I didn't deserve it (or so he told me). If I could just meet his expectations (which were ever changing and never attainable), I could finally gain the love and acceptance I was desperate to have.

I grew increasingly broken. I even tried to leave a few times. But every time, I'd end up right back where I was. More broken. More lost. And more isolated from my friends and family, who at this point didn't know what was happening in my relationship but saw enough red flags that they were rightly very concerned.

Eventually, he gave me a choice: walk away . . . or get married.

So, on a sunny November day in San Diego, I wore jeans and a long-sleeved black shirt and went with him to the courthouse—without telling any of our family members or friends. I honestly believed that getting married would fix things. After all, that's what he had been promising me.

I found out that night, however, that nothing was going to change. In fact, things were about to get worse. Much worse.

While the abuse and infidelity escalated, I was finally broken enough for a sliver of light to find its way into the darkness that was consuming and controlling my life.

There wasn't just one moment that led me to this place but a cumulation of many moments. And no doubt the continual prayers of my parents and other loved ones played a part—loved ones who at this point had no idea where I was living or whether

I was even alive. The reality is that even when we walk—or in my case *run*—away, God never stops His kind and loving pursuit. He really does leave the ninety-nine to pursue the one and, with gentleness, kindness, empathy, and grace, make Himself known. He provides a way out. He provides hope. We just need to choose to say yes.

My yes came one dark night in December. After another fight that left me afraid for my emotional and physical safety, I found myself at a breaking point. But that night, instead of Adam pretending nothing had happened and leaving me alone to "calm down" while he played video games, he did something unusual. He left.

After hearing the door close behind him, I did something I'd never done before. I asked God to help me. My prayer was simple, but it came from the bottom of my heart: *God, if You're real, get me out safely.*

Ten minutes later, God answered in the form of the arrival of one of Adam's friends. He was one of the few people who not only knew where we lived but also what was going on in our relationship. After confirming Adam wasn't home, he told me that he had shown up to talk to me. He looked me in the eyes and said, "Kari, I can't watch what's happening anymore. You need to know that you deserve better. I have a safe place for you to stay if you want it. Just pack up some stuff and stay there as long as you need."

That night I said yes to the way out before me.

That was the first moment I realized that God wasn't just an apathetic figurehead in the sky with no real interest in my life aside from demanding my perpetual and unquestioning obedience. That night, for the first time, I met a loving, deeply relational God who cared enough about a young woman who had walked away from Him and her family to find her in a sketchy apartment in middle-of-nowhere Arizona and give her a way out.

That night I said yes to the way out before me. And it began a journey of little yeses that eventually led me away from that relationship and into a place of healing, hope, and restoration. Of allowing God, not others, to determine my identity. Of choosing to receive not only God's blessing but also that of my parents when they gave it to me as I returned home. You'll read more about that moment with my parents later in this book.

Let me close with this: You may be reading this having walked through something so challenging that it's made you question your worth or even left you wondering if you really deserve the Blessing at all. Or you've done something that's created feelings of shame and left you feeling like there's no way this could really be for you.

I want to stop right now and tell you that no matter what's happened to you, no matter what you've done, *you are loved.* You're valuable. God's love and the Blessing are still available to you, and they're waiting for you to grab them with both hands and let them heal and transform the broken and shameful pieces of your life into something whole and beautiful that only God can create.

Nothing you've done or ever will do can separate you from His love. And nothing that's happened *to you* can separate you either (see Romans 8:35-39).

I understand the shame. I understand the challenge of accepting what feels so foreign or even undeserved. But just as God found me in that apartment that night, He's here with you today. He's asking for a little yes, a yes that says, *Okay, Lord, if You're real, I'm ready.* My prayer is that as you read this chapter and the ones that follow you will choose to say yes to the opportunities He puts before you to experience His love, redemption, and blessing.

The reality is that the opposite of the Blessing is the curse. And abuse is absolutely a powerful and life-changing curse. Abuse was so powerful that it erased the elements of the Blessing that I had experienced growing up. It even threatened to erase my future. But

God is stronger than abuse. And through Jesus, all the hurt and curse of that season in my life began to be reversed.

That process of reversal is what we're going to focus on in the next section of this book. We're going to look at a number of things we can do right now to reverse the curse. And we pray that as you read you will experience the healing love and blessing of Jesus on every page. God is ready. We only need to whisper, "Yes."

Good and evil both increase at compound interest. That is why the little decisions you and I make every day are of such infinite importance. The smallest good act today is the capture of a strategic point from which, a few months later, you may be able to go on to victories you never dreamed of.

Remember, we Christians think man lives for ever. Therefore, what really matters is those little marks or twists on the central, inside part of the soul which are going to turn it, in the long run, into a heavenly or a hellish creature.

C. S. LEWIS, *Mere Christianity*

PART THREE

SEVEN SMALL STEPS THAT CAN BEGIN TO CHANGE EVERYTHING

Someone once said that football is a game where fifty-five thousand people who are desperately in need of exercise sit watching twenty-two people who are desperately in need of rest. We know you've been an active participant in reading this book so far. But now it's your time to get down on the field and join in the game.

In past chapters, we've shared insights we've gained from working with many hundreds of people who have missed the Blessing. And you've read our personal stories, how we went from missing to receiving God's blessing and the blessing of others.

Now it's time for your story, your journey, to take center stage.

To do that, since we're not face-to-face with you, we'd like to coach you the way we would if we were able to meet.

And while it may seem surprising, what we advise is that you start taking small steps. Don't aim for massive leaps or huge changes overnight.

In his quote above, C. S. Lewis captures clearly why small things matter in big ways. If, like us, you're from the US, you've probably grown up focused on that one huge, grand-slam home run that can win the game. We celebrate that magical fingertip catch, with both feet barely down in bounds, that clinches the championship just as time runs out.

But Jesus talked about being "faithful in a very little thing" (Luke 16:10). About how a person's small, faithful steps lead to being rewarded much.

In these next several chapters, we'll encourage you to take seven such small steps. None may seem earth-shattering. But they're the very things we'd be coaching you to do on Zoom or in our office or at a conference. These small steps can help you move from missing to receiving, giving, and living the Blessing.

And He was saying,

"How shall we picture the kingdom of God?"

MARK 4:30

CHAPTER 16

GAINING (OR REGAINING) A CLEAR PICTURE OF A LOVING FATHER AND SON

Where do you go to get pictures of what it means to bless if you've never seen them in your daily experience? That's our first small step. Many of us didn't have a person we could tag along behind, go on trips with, or watch how he did life well, how she blessed others just in her everyday life.

Those missing pictures of blessing make it harder for us to understand what to do in many settings. How do you step toward others, not away? What does it look like to treat strangers well, to build relationships, to deal with challenges?

Therefore, an important starting point when you've grown up without the Blessing is to fill in some of those missing-blessing pictures.

We'll look at five of these pictures in this chapter and first step. But there are many more we could look at. Each of them is as close as your nearest Bible.

Wait . . . we're going to start a journey to deal with a problem this big with a Bible study? There's got to be something more helpful than that.

To answer that, let's consider someone who likewise questioned whether something small and seemingly unrelated could really be of help in facing a big problem. We find his story in the Bible, in 2 Kings 5. This great person had a big problem that he wanted solved *now*. Let's jump into the story:

> Now Naaman, commander of the army of the king of Aram, was a great man in the view of his master, and eminent, because by him the LORD had given victory to Aram. The man was also a valiant warrior, but afflicted with leprosy.
>
> 2 KINGS 5:1

That last statement, *but afflicted with leprosy*, didn't mean what it does today. There was no salve then, no medicine, no hope when someone became a leper. Naaman may have held a great position and been a great warrior and great person, but he had been handed a death sentence.

Then a little servant girl in his home spoke up. She was a captured Israelite, and while no one else could see any hope for Namaan's slow, defiling death sentence, she did. She told his grieving wife, "If only my master were with the prophet who is in Samaria! Then he would cure him of his leprosy" (2 Kings 5:3).

That would be like saying today, "Your husband has stage four pancreatic cancer that has spread everywhere in his body? *No worries.* There's someone near where I used to live who can absolutely heal him right now. Just go see him, and *poof*—it'll be gone."

If you've never been totally out of options when trying to help a loved one with no chance of living, then relying on the advice of a little girl might seem ridiculous. But Naaman's wife was indeed out of options, and she took the girl's words to heart. So did her husband, and so did the king whom Naaman had served so well.

So off went Naaman with his king's blessing, with horses and soldiers and animals loaded with gold, silver, and expensive garments. He showed up at the palace of the king of Israel. After all, Naaman was a great person who served a king. So he forgot the preacher and went to Israel's king. He wanted to go someplace significant, like Mayo Clinic and its top physician, not to some small-town general practitioner.

The king, of course, couldn't help. Naaman got redirected to that small-town prophet. And when he showed up with all his horsemen and gifts, the prophet didn't even come out to greet him. He sent out a servant, and it was his words Naaman had to believe and follow if he was to live.

"Go and wash in the Jordan seven times, and your flesh will be restored to you and you will be clean," he was told (2 Kings 5:10).

But as we might expect of a so-called great man, that sounded like total nonsense. Go wash in a green and brown river? Forget that. Or as we read in Scripture,

> Naaman was furious and went away, and he said,
> "Behold, I thought, 'He will certainly come out to me,
> and stand and call on the name of the LORD his God,
> and wave his hand over the site and cure the leprosy.' Are
> Abanah and Pharpar, the rivers of Damascus, not better
> than all the waters of Israel? Could I not wash in them
> and be clean?" So he turned and went away in a rage.
> 2 KINGS 5:11-12

Again, that makes total sense if you're the best of the best. But thankfully for Naaman, he had some special and brave friends. Those friends told him, "My father, had the prophet told you to do some great thing, would you not have done it? How much more then, when he says to you, 'Wash, and be clean'?" (2 Kings 5:13).

In short, "You'd have done something big. *But what if you're wrong?* Maybe you should do something small."

And Naaman did, and he was miraculously healed.

Naaman wanted to micromanage what he thought would bring life, and he wanted something big and dramatic. But it is often the small things that can bring big changes.

So if you missed the Blessing or endured a season in which it was erased, the first small step is for you to start filling in some missing pictures. You haven't had someone live out the Blessing in front of you, and you need to see how blessing someone really can and should take place.

That's just what God's Word does. It gives us pictures of a God who blesses. It gives us pictures of *Jesus*, who blesses. You may have missed all five elements of the Blessing, but we're about to look at five pictures that can fill in many of the holes in your life.

You haven't had someone live out the Blessing in front of you, and you need to see how blessing someone really can and should take place.

We'll see Jesus giving us a picture of what a loving heavenly Father looks like. Then we'll look at four pictures that Jesus gave us of Him blessing others. Each one can help fill in what we never saw in a home that withheld the Blessing. Looking at God's Word is a small step, but it's a great starting point to knowing how to bless.

Someone Who Welcomes You Home

This picture is tucked away in Luke 15. It's a parable, but in sharing it, Jesus gives us a picture of what His Father is like. If you've struggled with having a clear picture of what your heavenly Father is like—what any loving, blessing father is like—let's let Jesus describe Him.

Jesus was speaking to the Pharisees about all the joy there is in heaven when just one wayward person turns around and comes home to his waiting Father. The story is familiar.

The prodigal son decided he wanted to see the world and sow some wild oats. But when the money from his inheritance ran out, he was destitute in a distant land, and the only job he could get was in a pigsty. What brought him to his senses and put him on the road back home was a picture of his father's generosity: "How many of my father's hired laborers have more than enough bread, but I am dying here from hunger!" (Luke 15:17).

As the son made his way home, his father spotted him. Take a look at the picture of how the father responded, and get ready for a lesson on giving and living the Blessing:

> When he was still a long way off, his father saw him and felt compassion for him, and ran and embraced him and kissed him. And the son said to him, "Father, I have sinned against heaven and in your sight; I am no longer worthy to be called your son." But the father said to his slaves, "Quickly bring out the best robe and put it on him, and put a ring on his finger and sandals on his feet; and bring the fattened calf, slaughter it, and let's eat and celebrate; for this son of mine was dead and has come to life again; he was lost and has been found." And they began to celebrate.
>
> LUKE 15:20-24

If you missed the Blessing, a lot of it is right here in this picture. Spoken words of love and affirmation. As we talked about with attaching high value, the father's eyes searching for his son. The delight when he saw him. The heart that went out to him. The legs that ran to him. There's the appropriate, meaningful touch in the arms that embraced him and the lips that kissed him. There's the heart that attached high value to someone who had been sleeping with pigs the day before. The love that pictured a special future for this child who had been lost and was now found. And the genuine commitment that didn't just take the wayward son back *conditionally*, on probation, or make him wait until his angry, pharisaic older brother finally approved or felt that the prodigal had done enough or suffered enough or been humbled enough.

That very hour, the prodigal was given a robe and a ring—signs of a family relationship. Signs that he was welcomed home, that he was still an important part of the family. It's all there. And it's all for us, too.

That picture is particularly for you and all of us who never received a blessing from our fathers. Never received the attention, the understanding. Never received the compassion, the embraces, the forgiveness, the restoration, the love, the joy, the being welcomed home, the delight showing, unmistakably, in a father looking at his child.

The prodigal son in Luke 15 didn't need to go to Disneyland to find the most wonderful place on earth. He just needed to go home to his father's love.

Could there be a father like that in all the universe?

There is, and Jesus has given us a picture of not just who He is *but also of who we can be empowered to become with His love.* We, too, can be people of blessing like our heavenly Father.

Someone once said that a child is not likely to find a father in God unless he finds something of God in his father. I (John) never found that in my biological father. But I did find it in my spiritual father, Doug Barram. He showed me this picture in God's Word and many others, pictures I needed in order to see my heavenly Father more clearly.

A child is not likely to find a father in God unless he finds something of God in his father.

I (Kari) am blessed to have a father who has shown me this picture of our heavenly Father more times than I dare to count. Let me tell you about one such time, because you may need to hear the words my father spoke. Those words mirror the father in the parable above and our heavenly Father now.

After the Lord showed up powerfully for me in my sketchy apartment that night and I began the process of healing, I, like the prodigal son, had to confront the hurt and pain I had caused others. I wasn't just reeling from the effects of abuse; I was also shrouded in shame. Shame for the choices I'd made. Shame for things that had happened or been done to me. Shame that my life had reached the crisis point it was at.

I was given an incredible opportunity to confront some of this hurt, pain, and shame when a friend connected me with a church in Tacoma, Washington, that was doing a one-month program aimed at helping broken young adults like me find hope and healing in Jesus. And now I was finally on my way home to Arizona. I needed to make some big decisions about what my future held.

I remember sitting on the plane and being excited to see my family for the first time in years. I was no longer afraid of what reception I might receive, and I was proud of how far I had come in such a short time. That is, until I showed up at my parents' doorstep.

I knew instantly that something was wrong. The exuberant welcome I expected was nonexistent. My parents looked worn out, tired, and more than a little brokenhearted.

"Is everything okay? What happened?" I finally asked, not able to stand the silence.

That's when they told me. Earlier, my ex-husband had shown up at their door. And while I won't go into details, it was not a pleasant or safe conversation. They not only had to deal with issues related to their safety, but they also learned about years' worth of lies I'd told and horrible choices I'd made. Some were completely true as stated by my ex-husband. Others he had twisted and used to intentionally harm my parents in a way that only a true manipulator can do.

Needless to say, it was about as bad a situation as you can imagine. And while the Lord was kind in His protection of their physical safety, they were still processing the pain, fear, and emotional toll that had been thrown upon them without warning.

They had survived the emotional attack. But what would it do to our relationship?

I looked down at my packed bag, thinking it was a good thing I was already packed and ready to go. Surely this was the moment—the moment when my parents had finally reached their limit. When they were finally going to tell me they no longer loved me or wanted anything to do with me. When they wanted me out of their lives forever.

The clash of those emotions on their doorstep nearly broke me. Here I was, feeling better, more alive and more hopeful than I had in years . . . and now here I was at the lowest point I could ever imagine. How could I get back up on my feet now? How could I possibly move forward?

As I grabbed my bag to leave, my dad stepped forward and kindly put his hand on my shoulder. "Kari, look at me," he said gently, his voice broken and full of emotion.

I forced myself to look up and hold his gaze.

"Kari, I need you to know something. What happened today doesn't define who you are. *Please hear me when I tell you it's not about where you've been; it's about where you're going.*"

And he and my mom both gave me their blessing.

They told me that I was still their daughter. That they still loved me. That they still saw the incredible future God had ahead for me. And most important to me at that moment, that they were not done with me or our relationship.

I want to be clear here. Our relationship wasn't fixed in that moment. A lot of work and healing still needed to be done. I still had a lot of trust to rebuild. And boundaries still needed to be held and honored.

But that moment set me free. My parents still loved me. Even after all that. After all they had found out. After the dangerous and painful situation my choices had put them in. After all that, *they still chose me.* And they still believed that who I was did not need to be determined by my past choices but could be redefined by God's grace, redemption, and promises moving forward.

I share that story because I know I needed my parents' blessing to really move forward.

I may not know the darkest pieces of your story. But God does. And as my parents came face-to-face with mine that day, I desperately needed to hear the words *It's not about where you've been; it's about where you're going. You are not your past. You are not beyond help, hope, or love. Nothing is too big for God to still choose you or for others to choose you.*

So if you're like me, please hear this: *Beloved, it's not about where you've been. It's about where you're going. You are not your past. You are not beyond help, hope, or love. Nothing is too big for God. He still chooses you. And He always will. You are worthy of love, forgiveness, and the incredible future He has for you. We choose you too. And we pray that as you continue on this journey you will experience the healing love and acceptance of others as well.*

Someone Seeing Great Value in You

The next four pictures show us how Jesus blessed people. In each one, it's like we're being welcomed to walk alongside Him and see how, in different ways and different situations, He stepped into different lives. To each He brought home the Blessing in a way they needed.

That's something I (John) never had with my father—pictures of him in different settings. I never saw how he acted around a crowd, in a business meeting, or at a sports event. I had no pictures of what a father was supposed to look like.

But when I became a father, I decided that my kids wouldn't miss those pictures. So, early on, I vowed I would never go on an errand alone if possible. From the time our two daughters were old enough to jump in the car with me, I'd take one or both with me everywhere. To pick up paint. To drop off something at a friend's house. To do a grocery run for Cindy.

The girls probably felt like they saw too much of me at times. But what a tremendous time it was to build relationships. To talk in the car. To let them ask questions along the way. To do life with them.

Jesus was always taking time to engage with people. He met them where they were and stepped into their lives. Consider a story that's found in John 4, the picture of the woman He met at a well.

She came to the well at noon, the hottest part of the day, and that alone whispers something of her reputation. Most women would have come early in the morning or at dusk when it was cool. This woman had had five husbands, and she wasn't married to the man she was living with now. So she came midday to fill her jar, probably to avoid the gossip, the stares, and the fingers pointed in her direction.

Jesus was always taking time to engage with people.

When she met Jesus at that well and He asked for a drink, she was startled.

"How is it that You, though You are a Jew, are asking me for a drink, though I am a Samaritan woman?" (John 4:9).

It struck her as odd, partly because He was a Jew, and the Jews had no dealings with the Samaritans. Besides that, He was a man, and men had little social contact with women. Yet to her and to her alone He gave one of the greatest revelations in all of Scripture: that "God is spirit, and those who worship Him must worship in spirit and truth" (John 4:24).

The short conversation they had at that well changed her life. It blessed her to know that someone like Jesus would talk with someone of her reputation. And if you read the account in John, you'll see that it's a real conversation they had—not a monologue but a dialogue. Not a sermon but genuine interaction.

Jesus showing up in her world, meeting her where she was, talking with her about her life, and treating her with dignity and respect creates a truly beautiful picture of the way God comes to each of us. *He meets us at the well where we are.* Engages us in conversation. Treats us with respect. Moves us closer and closer to Him.

Doug Barram dropped lots of pictures like that into my life. He was an adult, yet he showed up in a high school world, meeting me on the football field or in the gym. He talked with me about my life, treated me with dignity and respect, and moved me closer and closer to the well of living water.

I remember one time in particular. He took seven of us who were in his Campaigner Bible study out to breakfast. We were all seniors, and he had led each of us to Christ. He wanted to get us all together before we left for college or whatever we had decided to do with our lives. After we finished eating, he had each of us say what our goals and dreams were for the future.

My brother Jeff said he wanted to be a doctor, which came as a shock to no one. He had decided on that track back when we were five. One of the other guys wanted to become a commercial pilot. He would go on to get his pilot's license in a few short months. Another wanted to go into business in some way. Another intended to become a professional photographer.

When it was my turn, I said I wanted to get my doctorate, write books, and help people who were hurting. Everybody at the table laughed—except two people. The others laughed because I was a terrible student. I had crawled across the finish line to graduate high school. Later, I got turned down by all the four-year colleges I applied to and went to junior college on academic probation. Perhaps there was a pattern: I'd get into Texas Christian University, then seminary, and then into my doctoral program *on probation.*

With my academic track record, everyone had good reason to laugh. The two people who didn't laugh were my brother, who has always been wonderfully supportive, and Doug. He believed I could do it. He treated me with dignity and respect that day. He told the other guys to put a sock in the laughter. He said he wouldn't be surprised a bit if I ended up helping people like that.

I'm not sure how or why Doug insisted he saw something in me that day when the others were so merciless in their laughter and dismissal of my dreams. But I never forgot the picture of this adult meeting with a bunch of high school kids around a table, engaging us in dialogue about our lives, and treating us all with dignity and respect.

We need people in our lives who can see high value in us. As my mom did. As Doug did. As Jesus did and does today.

If this is your story, please hear us say that you are valuable. Your wants, needs, and desires are important. We believe in you. And we know that God has an incredible future ahead for you.

Know that God has an incredible future ahead for you. This is your invitation to dream again with Him.

This is your invitation to dream again with Him. To let Him access the desires of your heart. The wells may have run dry. Offer it all. And allow Him to bless you with His living water in return.

The woman at the well was so changed by her encounter with the Savior that she went back to her town, and her story, passion, and new life changed her entire village. We believe your story will change the lives of many too. You are valuable and hold great value to the Lord and to us.

Someone Going out of His Way to Serve You

This picture is mounted in the Scriptures in John 13. In the upper room on the night of His arrest, Jesus was celebrating a last meal with His disciples. Before the meal, much to their surprise, He washed their feet. It was the duty of a servant to greet guests with a basin of water and a towel. To take off their sandals and wash the dirt from their feet. "[I] did not come to be served, but to serve," Jesus had said earlier (Mark 10:45). This is one of the pictures that shows us that He meant it.

Think about dirty feet and a large bowl of water, water that's getting dirtier with every disciple's foot washed. The teacher going out of His way to do that for His students.

And know that Jesus still does this for you and me. He stops to serve us. To cleanse us. To refresh us. To make us feel like guests in His presence. What a picture of blessing, then and now!

Can you see how Jesus treated other people like honored guests? Once again, all the elements of the Blessing show up, this time as Jesus stoops and pours water over His disciples' feet. Appropriate, meaningful touch. Attaching high value. Genuine commitment.

If you think back to when we looked at homes that withheld blessing, you'll remember that the reason many of us never saw someone serving us in love is that the people withholding the Blessing never received it! With their own need for an element of the Blessing so deep, they didn't have the fullness, even the capacity, to bless. They were so focused on what they missed, on what they needed, there was no room to be a servant to others. But the one who wants to be the greatest, Jesus said, is the servant of all (see Mark 10:44)!

I (Kari) have a "foot-washing" picture from my dad, who has blessed me with many Christlike pictures over my life. It's a picture I have of coming home to apples and peanut butter.

As I said earlier, the pictures I remember from high school are anything but warm and happy. I transferred to a private Christian school for my freshman year. However, instead of being met by loving kids who were excited to have a new classmate, I was greeted by a group of kids who had grown up together and were not excited to welcome in outsiders.

What started out as a tough transition became four years of rejection and sometimes outright hostility. I wrote before of the rumors, the spray-painting of our house, the lack of invitations to social events. But I'm thankful for a choice my dad made, one that cost him something.

Just as it cost Jesus something to wash His disciples' feet, blessing others often has a cost. This isn't necessarily a financial cost but might be the cost of time, energy, and/or effort. Or in my dad's case, the cost was some snacks and a good chunk of sleep.

While I didn't have a ton of friends, I did make the varsity cheer squad as a freshman and stay on it through my senior year. This meant that there were a lot of out-of-town football and basketball games and late nights practicing for competitions. And every night I got home late, whether it was from a game, a practice, or a night out with friends—each time I pulled into the driveway—I always saw the light on in the kitchen.

I'd walk into the house, and I'd find my dad waiting up, no matter what time it was, with my favorite snack, apple slices and peanut butter.

As I'd sit down to have my snack, Dad would ask questions about my day or the night I'd had. Some conversations were challenging and full of tears. Others were full of laughter or a fun story about something that had happened. But no matter what, good or bad, I had someone who sat there with me, often in the middle of the night, and listened. He shared encouragement when I needed it. He was excited to see me come home. Even if none of those kids were excited to see me at school that day, I got to end my day with someone who was genuinely glad to see me, even on my worst day.

That wasn't the only time my dad stayed up late to bless me. He stayed up late to help me finish my term papers by driving me to Kinko's at two in the morning to make copies of all my sources. (This was before online tools or submission options.) He stayed up late to keep me company as I crammed for a test the next day. Even if he was just reading a book in the same room, his presence provided a sense of hope that I could stay awake for a few more minutes and maybe, just maybe, pass that impossible physics test.

Did your dad ever sleep? Honestly, if I wasn't sleeping, I really don't think he slept much throughout those challenging high school years. I remember asking him one time, "Dad, do you ever hate being up with me so late?"

His eyes misted over with his reply. "I asked my mom that same question once, and I'm going to share with you the same thing she said to me. I can always go back to sleep. I won't always be here to talk with you."

It was his way of serving, his way of washing my feet, his way of saying that I mattered, that he was excited about what was important to me. Even if it was just providing my favorite snack after a horrible day, driving me to Kinko's, or staying up with me when I was stressed.

Again, that's what many of us have missed when we've missed the Blessing. Someone taking us seriously. Someone being willing to sacrifice to serve us, even if it meant losing sleep. Jesus showed how serving others links powerfully with blessing them. That's a picture we need as we get started in blessing others.

If that was missing for you, we want you to know that Jesus is with you, cares for you, and will never give up on you.

Someone Seeing Your Potential

This next picture is found in Matthew 16. When you read the passage, it looks as if Jesus took a brash and impulsive fisherman, asked him one question, and then, on the basis of his answer, commissioned him to lead His church. That's not exactly how most people would pick a leader.

Actually, it wasn't Peter's answer that impressed Jesus. It's what He saw in Peter's potential. Where others saw only the sharp and abrasive edges of a rock, Jesus saw a foundation. Where others saw unpredictability, Jesus saw stability. Where others saw the rough hands of a fisherman, Jesus saw hands that would hold the keys of the Kingdom of Heaven. He saw Peter not for who he was but for who he was to become.

What a picture Peter was blessed with! What a picture we're all blessed with when we're told that we have been predestined to be conformed to the image of Christ (Romans 8:29) and that He who began a good work in us will bring it to completion (Philippians 1:6)! What potential He sees in us!

I (Kari) remember a significant time when someone saw potential in me, even though I couldn't yet see it in myself. I was knee-deep in my relationship with my then husband and virtually estranged from my entire family. However, God was about to use some old tires to remind me who I was and *whose* I was.

One morning, I received a text from my dad saying he had received an email telling him my car was due for some new tires. He followed it up with "If you meet me at the tire shop, I'll buy you a new set."

I'm ashamed to say it, but I really didn't want to go. It wasn't because I didn't want to see my dad. I didn't want to have to talk about how I was, where I was living, and what was really going on. And even more, I knew the aftermath of seeing my family would be horrible. The way my now ex would treat me when I got home was bad enough to make me think twice even about free tires. But the money won out. And that day, God's blessing did too.

I went to the tire shop, and Dad came up to me holding a piece of paper. He handed it to me and told me to read it when he left.

Realizing it was probably some heartbreaking plea to come home or questions about where I was, I almost didn't take it from him. But I did. And when he left, I opened it up and was shocked to find not a lecture, a sermon, or lines of accusation but a list.

A list of ten truths about who I was.

Ten character traits my dad saw in me. Ten things that made me special, unique, and valuable.

Ten things I honestly didn't see in myself. Things like "You have a special future ahead of you. You are incredibly talented at writing in a way that blesses others. You are courageous and caring." And, maybe best of all, "You are incredibly loved and valuable."

I went home that day with the list still in my purse. And while the aftermath was every bit as bad as I had expected, something different began to happen.

My ex would say or do something incredibly harmful and abusive, and I'd find myself going into the bathroom and pulling out that list.

The first million times I read the words and thought, *There's no way any of this is true about me. After all, someone I love just told me I'm the complete opposite of everything here. There's no way this list can be true.*

Then slowly something began to shift.

I'd read it and begin to think, *Gosh, I want these things to be true of me.*

And one day, almost a year later, I pulled out the words and thought, *Maybe these things* can *be true about me.*

I'm proud to say that two years after receiving that list, I was able to hand it back to my dad and tell him with a smile that I believed every single thing he had written. I told him God had helped me heal to a point where I now not only knew the unique way He had made me but for the first time in years was actually living in that truth as well.

One day, almost a year later, I pulled out the words and thought, Maybe these things can be true about me.

Needless to say, that was a day of deep celebration for both of us, and for my mom and sister as well, who had each added to the list as Dad had written it.

Maybe you're like me when I received that list—in a place

where you don't know if there's really anything good about you because there has previously been so much negative said and done, so much subtraction. Or maybe you're at a place where you want it to be true. But perhaps today is the day when you finally believe that the words of life, blessing, and truth are real for you as well.

No matter where you are today, I hope I get the chance to hear from you at some point that, like me, you also believe the powerful words of truth God says about you—about your worth, your value, and the unique and incredible way He has made you.

If you're reading this because a loved one is hurting, I pray your words of blessing will have the same impact that my family's did for me at a time when I needed them most.

You never know whom you're going to bless like Jesus when you point out for someone a special future you see for him or her.

In my memory, that picture—that tire store I walked into, my dad paying for the tires and handing me that list—is as clear as the day it was taken, and so dear.

Someone Making Time to Bless You

Let's look at one more picture of how Jesus took blessing people to such an amazing level and why we should, if we're serious about moving from missing to giving the Blessing, look at Him. This is one of my favorites. You can find it framed in Luke 8.

Jesus was on His way to heal a dying twelve-year-old girl, the daughter of a synagogue official named Jairus. As He walked, the crowds pressed against Him. The scene was intense. A girl's life was at stake. An eager crowd packed around Him. And then a woman with constant bleeding pushed through the crowd, thinking, *If I can just get close enough to touch His garment, that will be enough.* Finally, she did get close enough and touched the fringe of His garment. Barely a tug. But she knew she had touched Him, and He felt it. He stopped.

He was sensitive to the touch because it was a touch of faith. He called to her, waiting as she finally came, trembling, and fell down before Him. And ever so tenderly, He told her, "Daughter, your faith has made you well; go in peace" (Luke 8:48).

It's one of our favorite pictures because it shows us a lot about the way Jesus lived out the Blessing. We see how sensitive Jesus is to the slightest touch of faith we can extend to Him. We don't have to have the right words, the right timing, or the right anything.

All we have to do is reach out to Him.

And He stops for us.

When everything was pointing in one direction, Jesus was willing to see and acknowledge another. It's not that His original goal wasn't important. A child's life was at stake, after all. So Jesus shouldn't have been bothered—but He chose to recognize someone else who needed His help and blessing.

Think about a child in your family. The one who wants a hug from you before you have to walk out the door to that important meeting. Or your spouse needing help with the baby right in the middle of the fourth quarter with your team struggling to get ahead.

That's no time to be interrupted! Or is it?

Who was there in your life who took the time, time he or she didn't have, to do something that said, "I love you"? That said, "Giving you a hug is more valuable to me then fifty meetings"? Or as my (Kari's) dad said, "I can always go back to sleep."

The way Jesus noticed the small things is a great tutorial on how to be a person of blessing. And in many ways, it reminds me (John) of the picture of when I first heard those words from my mom.

During my senior year in high school, Jeff and I had a ritual we went through with several of our friends. After we dropped off our Saturday-night dates (if we had dates), we'd all meet at the local Jack in the Box at eleven o'clock sharp. Being high school boys, athletes, and having, as Mom said, "hollow legs," we were always ready to eat a second dinner. And an hour was plenty of time to wolf down an entire menu of tacos, burgers, fries, and shakes before they kicked us out and closed the doors. That meant it was about midnight when Jeff and I arrived home for another ritual.

We'd walk in, head down the hall to the last room on the left, open the door, and wake up our mother. With all the medicines she took, she would usually be conked out by eight thirty or nine at the latest. Without trying to be quiet, we'd both walk into her room and flop down on either side of her.

It was pitch-dark. We never turned on the light. We'd nudge her until we were sure she was actually awake, and then we'd start to talk. We'd talk about our evening, our dates if we'd had them, the movies we saw, the people we met. The conversation would drift to what our weeks had been like, what had gone well, what hadn't. We'd end up sharing our dreams, telling each other the details of our lives, all there in the dark on our mom's bed.

Then one Saturday night, months after this ritual had begun, a thought struck me. "Mom?" I asked. "Does it bother you, us waking you up so late to talk?"

"Boys," she said, patting us in the dark, "I can always go back to sleep. But I won't always have you boys here to talk to. Wake me up anytime."

And I knew she meant it. She was sensitive to the touch of her two teenage boys who wanted to talk at midnight. Even when she was asleep. Even when she had to get up and talk with us when we were ready to talk. Even when she had to get up early the next day. She was never so tired or so pressured that she couldn't feel that touch in the dark. She always had time to listen. To choose to bless us. *Always.*

There you have five pictures from Scripture that can start to fill the holes in your past if you missed the Blessing. We started your journey away from missing the Blessing and toward becoming a person of blessing with the Bible because God's Word never fails. It never returns void, it is never untrue, and it's always ready for you to open it up in the middle of a dark night or on a very difficult day. Just take one picture at a time. When you do, you'll see the blessing that Jesus, the heavenly Father, and the Holy Spirit are to you and how you, in turn, can begin to be a blessing in someone else's life.

This memorial with its wall of names, becomes
a place of quiet reflection, and a tribute to those
who served their nation in difficult times. All
who come here can find it a place of healing.

BRENT ASHABRANNER, *Always to Remember:*
The Story of the Vietnam Veterans Memorial

CHAPTER 17

THE BEGINNING OF THE END OF YOUR WAR

Having gained those pictures of a loving God, let's now look at a second step we'd like you to take. It's small, though not easy. But it's a step that can place something in your home, office, or garage that can remind you of the day your healing began—the day the worst part of the battle over your missing of the Blessing ended. The day when you, before the Lord, decided that peace could start. Let us explain by telling you about how such a step was once taken to honor the fallen and help heal our nation.

At a Time of Great Struggle

The Vietnam War was the foreign conflict of my (John's) youth. The official count of American combatants who died there is 58,220.[1] Yet several years after that unpopular war ended, there was still tremendous pain and upheaval. The hurt was such that those years had gone by with nothing having been done to honor either the living or the dead who had served in the war.

One soldier who fought in Vietnam was Jan Scruggs. While he was studying at American University after the war, he came up with the idea that America needed some kind of memorial to the men and women who had died in Vietnam. But it wasn't until two years later, in 1979, that the idea took hold of him.

Scruggs had gone to see the movie *The Deer Hunter*. It's a soul-searching movie about a group of soldiers who go to Vietnam and the tragic struggle for several of them after they come home. The movie bothered him so much that he couldn't sleep. He tossed and turned all night with flashbacks of his own combat experiences, including horrible memories of a mortar attack that had left twelve of his friends dead.

The next morning, he told his wife that he was going to build a memorial *and that all the names of the dead would be on it.* That was his vision.

After a lengthy process of raising funds, obtaining permission to proceed, and choosing a design, construction began on two walls of black granite to reflect the sky and bear the name of every lost service member.

When it was completed and dedicated, an amazing thing happened. One by one, as people began spotting the names of their loved ones, they reached out their hands to touch them. Fingers strained to touch the etchings of a life, the name of someone they loved. And all the memories came back.

People wept. People embraced. People talked and prayed. After a decade of silence and shame since the war ended, the pain and anguish began to spill from America's soul. And that day the nation's deep wound began to heal.

Then people started bringing mementos to the wall and leaving them there. They brought so many that a warehouse had to be found to store them all. The phenomenon continues to this day. About a third of the mementos are military in nature—ribbons, medals, identification tags, things like that. About a third of them are written material—cards, letters, poems. The other third is a miscellaneous collection of toys, books, phonograph records, and such. Each item is labeled with an inventory number along with the number of the panel on the wall where it was found.

The curator of these mementos in the 1980s was a man named David Guynes. When someone once asked him why all these things were saved, he opened a cabinet full of toys and took out a small, worn teddy bear. "This was one of the early mementos left at the memorial," he said.

A mother and father whose son's name is on the wall put it there. They left a greeting card, too, and a photograph of a 1955 car. Newspaper articles were written about the bear, and the parents identified themselves. They were interviewed on Ted Koppel's *Nightline* television program. They said they had bought the bear for their son in 1938, when he was a baby. They wanted to return it to him. The car in the photo was his first car.

He continued:

Most museums, most curators, carefully select what is to make up their collection. That's not the case here. We must collect everything. There are so many questions, so many mysteries, in these [memorabilia]. So many stories are in them, so much feeling, emotion, heartache. What can be learned about America and Americans from these things they have brought? Altogether, these materials make up a very important part of the story of the Vietnam War.[2]

In *The Winds of War*, Herman Wouk wrote that "the beginning of the end of war lies in remembrance."[3] That was true for all the Vietnam veterans who had come back from the war but who were still living with it, still sleeping with it, still fighting it, still trying to drink it away, drug it away, pray it away. For many of them, the memorial was the beginning of the end of the war that had raged inside them with intensity and had claimed staggering losses.

The same thing that moved a nation's heart to heal is what we want to talk to you about in this chapter. That's the power of an object, the power of a picture. But before I was ready to create such an object or picture, I had to meet someone first. I had to find a blessing that would help me end my war with my father.

Understanding

For me, a huge gift and blessing from God, and a major step in my healing from missing the Blessing, came when I began attending Texas Christian University (TCU) in Fort Worth, Texas.

I had transferred in as a junior. My first semester, I registered for an advanced English class. On the first day of class, the teacher assigned each of us a specific topic for a term paper. But this was 1972, not the present. There was no internet. There were no virtual libraries. You had to go inside an actual library to check out materials.

The subject the teacher assigned me required some extra effort. She said she had a good friend who was the research librarian at a rival school and her friend had loads of material on my subject. So she gave me a letter explaining things and told me to go to Dallas. Her friend would give me everything I needed for my research. Off I went to SMU—the dreaded Southern Methodist University, TCU's biggest rival at the time.

It's roughly a forty-minute drive from Fort Worth to Dallas. I arrived and found a place to park. The SMU campus is architecturally magnificent. I asked for directions and was pointed toward a stunning redbrick building called Fondren Library. After a brief stop at the circulation desk, I was off to find the research expert.

They'd told me to head down an aisle that led to a suite of

offices. Once I got there, I was to turn right and then go along the offices, and if I kept going straight, I would run right into the desk of the person I needed.

Off I went, and when I got to the offices, I saw that the glass door of the first office was open. Large letters on the window stopped me: "Robert M. Trent, Head Librarian."

Inside the office sat a distinguished-looking gentleman with stylish white hair. He was sitting behind a desk in a large leather chair, looking down, and writing something. To this day, I don't know why I did what I did next, though I believe the Lord knew what I was doing. Perhaps I'd done one too many Young Life skits. Or it might be because I'm an "Otter" in the animal personality test I helped create,[4] meaning that I'm usually friendly with others.

I had no idea I was related to anyone in Texas. And now I had just walked into my actual uncle's office!

I figured the man sitting in the chair had to be none other than Robert M. Trent, Head Librarian.

Robert M. *Trent*. Same last name.

So instead of walking by, I popped my head in his door and said, "Hey, Uncle Bob! I'm your long-lost nephew, John Trent from Arizona!"

I expected confusion or some kind of denial—some funny reaction or, worst case, just that I'd be told to get lost.

Instead, the man sat forward in his chair, suddenly alert.

"Are you Joe Trent's boy?" he asked.

My mouth dropped open. I couldn't believe it. At that point, I had only met my father twice in my life. I knew nothing about any relatives on his side of the family. I had no idea I was related to anyone in Texas. And now I had just walked into my actual uncle's office!

He invited me in and had me sit down. I quickly found out that he was really my *great*-uncle, my father's uncle. And while his first name was Robert, he went by his middle name, Max.

"Call me Max!" he said.

Not only was he my great-uncle, but it also turned out that my twin brother, Jeff, had been named after him! Jeffrey *Maxwell* Trent. I'd walked in on Jeff's namesake! But it was me, not Jeff, who was invited to go home with him for dinner that night.

That's where I met Aunt Sally, his wife, who was warm and gracious to an unexpected dinner guest and relative. That night, I would discover that they were both Ph.D.s from Columbia University in library science and that Uncle Max had been the head librarian at LSU for more than a decade. Now he was not only the head librarian of Fondren Library but also the director of all SMU libraries.

It was a wonderful evening. They had never had children and were beyond gracious. As a result of that night, I regularly got invited to their home during my two years at TCU and my four years at Dallas Theological Seminary. We'd sit down at dinner, and at every meal, I was also served insights and pictures and stories. Many missing pieces of my father's story came to light.

My father had four brothers, Max told me. They had all grown up on a farm, working from the time they got up in the morning until the time they went to bed. None of them were close to their dad (Uncle Max's brother), who looked at them more as hired hands than sons. Then, during the Dust Bowl, when times got really tough, my dad's father left the family—just as my father would leave our family one day when times got tough. His father had walked out on him. *I never knew that.*

My father and all his brothers ended up going to war. Two faced extended time in combat. One—my namesake, John (whom I never met)—served on a Navy ship in the Pacific, dodging kamikazes. My father fought island to island in the Pacific, trying to stay alive.

Uncle Max talked about my dad's experiences in the war—how he had been wounded three times and awarded several medals. I learned how, after being wounded for the third time, he had been flown home to recuperate. During that time, my father had lived with Max and Sally in New York while they were attending Columbia. Max told me about the terrible nightmares my dad had during that time and about how he began to do more and more self-medicating with alcohol, trying to drink away the terrible pictures that racked his dreams.

I had gone from hating my father before I became a Christian to now, as a believer—by God's grace and strength—having forgiven him. But I still knew nothing about him.

At my great-uncle's house during those dinners, I received a wonderful gift: the gift of understanding. The

He began to do more and more self-medicating with alcohol, trying to drink away the terrible pictures that racked his dreams.

gift of finding out some of the terrible losses my father had suffered. And, for the first time, the gift of having feelings of compassion for him.

I felt something of the ache he must have had for the dad he never really knew. Something of the torment that wouldn't let him rest from the terrible pictures of war. Something of the sorrows he carried within him that he tried to wash away with alcohol.

Gradually, the picture I had of him changed. It was no longer a black-and-white picture showing its faded age. Meeting Uncle Max had retinted it in my mind, humanizing it with color.

I had forgiven him, I think, at least the best I could for where I was, who I was. But it hadn't been easy. And it hadn't come all at once. Those nights at my great-uncle's helped a lot.

But there was something else I did several years later that now takes us to that second small step we want you to consider.

Declaring My War Over

Let's head back to the Vietnam Memorial. I remember when I went on a trip to Washington, DC, and saw the black granite for the first time. I found and traced the name of a friend I'd known who had died on his third tour of duty.

The loss I suffered in having missed my father's blessing is in no way comparable to the loss signified by those names on the wall. But at that wall I saw how an object could help heal the hurt of many. Being there made me think about my life and about a different war, World War II, which had damaged my father so badly.

I knew it was time for my war with missing the Blessing to stop.

When I got home, I started thinking about the war I'd been fighting within myself for years. The war that waged within me was far less intense, but still there were losses and pain, which is true for all of us who miss the Blessing.

And that's when I realized something else: For those of us who missed the Blessing, there needs to come a day when—*at least on our part*—we declare that the war is over. *That we are not going to fight or hate anymore.*

I realized then that the beginning of the end of my personal war was remembrance as well. And I knew I was tired of all the energy that I'd spent hating my father for years. I had expended near-constant emotional energy hating, while he had been indifferent at best. I had lost a lot of sleep over his not being there for us, but it hadn't bothered his sleep at all. At this time, he didn't even know the names of my children and didn't seem to care.

I was the one doing all the fighting! With myself. With God. With my father, when I didn't even know him.

That's when I realized my fighting had to end. In 1 John, the beloved disciple wrote that when we hate our brother (or in my case, my father), we can't see the love of God or the light of God (see 1 John 2:9-11).

It was time. I was tired of being dragged back into the darkness of hating my father for his never valuing or accepting or blessing me. I knew it was time for my war with missing the Blessing to stop. I wouldn't build a granite wall to commemorate it, but I could put together a shadow box.

The Verse Kept Haunting Me

I had been struggling to explain my relationship with my father to our two young daughters. They would ask why he rarely came over. But they also didn't know that there were times when he *had* come over but had been drinking so we'd set a boundary. He was welcome to come over, but only when he was sober.

Yet there was a verse—actually, that commandment we read earlier with a promise—that kept haunting me: "Honor your father and your mother, so that your days may be prolonged on the land which the Lord your God gives you" (Exodus 20:12).

At that stage of my life, I was tolerating my father. That was better than hating him. But how could I honor someone I couldn't trust to drive my kids in his car? Who had made a sum total of zero steps toward reconciliation?

Again, that's when I realized that *I had to end my part of the war.*

I knew enough now about my father's background from Uncle Max to know why he was so broken. So, after thinking and praying long and hard, I decided to do two things.

First, I decided to end the war. I declared before the Lord that officially on my part (I had no control over my father's decisions), the hostilities had ended. And I decided I needed to come up with a picture of something about my father that I *could* honor.

That's when the shadow box idea came to mind.

The idea hit me one Saturday when I was helping my father move apartments. Sometime earlier, I had saved a box he was throwing out. It was a miracle I had looked inside it instead of tossing it in the dumpster. It was filled with things that were priceless to me, like the Eisenhower jacket he wore coming home from the Pacific and a box with all the medals and ribbons he'd received. He would never talk about the war, but he was still fighting it inside, and he had decided that getting rid of the box would help get rid of more of the memories. On this day, I realized I still had that box in our garage. I recalled hearing about a company in Sun City, Arizona, that would take all the ribbons and medals someone had and put them into a shadow box. But they did much more. They would also request the service records of that man or woman. That way, they could fill in all the missing pieces. They could add in all the campaign ribbons, medals, and awards a person should have received but for whatever reason didn't. (With millions of soldiers coming home from World War II, many things were officially recorded but never awarded.) I decided to send them what I had.

Among other things, the box contained his blue combat infantry badge, two of his three Purple Hearts, and a Bronze Star. The company did a beautiful job of filling in the rest—the rank insignias, the three rows of ribbons, the medals.

Today, that shadow box hangs on a wall behind me as I write this. But when I first got it, it hung somewhere else.

There were many things I could not honor about my father. But this was one I could: his remarkable service to our country to help free the world from fascism. And this shadow box was my memorial wall—where I touched the past, where I was reminded that my war needed to end and that because I had God's blessing I could free myself from having to hate my father. I could bless him even if he couldn't do that for me. That box became and still is a source of healing.

So where did I hang it? For years, it hung above the piano, where our girls took lessons and practiced almost every day. I put it there for them to see. I explained as best I could all the ribbons, ranks, and medals and what they represented. I told them about their grandfather's service to our country. The wounds he'd suffered. The losses he'd had. They could be proud of what he'd done as they did their piano lessons.

Can You Think of Your Shadow Box?

This second small step may not seem so small. But that shadow box—that picture, that object—symbolized for me and reminds me today of the decision that my war, my hate, needed to end. And we'd encourage you to consider making a choice like that. Decide on a date when you say of your war, *Lord, enough is enough. I can't out-hate this person. I can't go back and change all the pictures. But I can say that on this day, as far as I can, with Your strength, the hate stops and healing begins.*

And then see if you can come up with something to remind you of that step you're taking to end your war, something you can place in your home or office.

Thanks to Uncle Max, I knew how much of my father had never come home from war. Thanks to God's grace, I'm able to look at the shadow box and be reminded that God forgives me for my anger and hate and calls me to forgive my father as well. It's also a way to remember all the sacrifices my father made and all Jesus has done for me.

It can be difficult to come up with something that honors someone who has never blessed you. It doesn't have to be a shadow box. It can be something small. One woman we worked with picked a date when her war ended and then, as a way of remembrance and to honor her father's memory, she went out and bought a small metal replica car. The car was inexpensive, a Matchbox miniature she'd found online. What made it meaningful was that it was the same year, same make, same model, and same color car as the one her father had driven when she and her brothers were kids.

The car didn't represent any great memories of family vacations or trips taken with her father. There had been none of those. Rather, she remembered her father driving their family to church, dropping her off with her mother and brothers, and going drinking with his friends (yes, on Sunday morning).

That's not a lot to honor, but it was what she came up with. He didn't stop them from going to church. He even drove them there. And it was at that small Presbyterian church near their home (and his bar) that her whole family (minus her father) started relationships with Jesus. So her "shadow box" was that small, light-blue 1980s Ford Escort Matchbox car.

Can you think of something God has done through, or that you can honor about, your non-blessing loved one that can help you take this next step toward forgiveness and away from missing the Blessing?

Down the way from the Vietnam Veterans Memorial is the Lincoln Memorial. Engraved on it are the words of Abraham Lincoln's second inaugural address to the nation. These are the final words of the address:

> With malice towards none, with charity for all, with firmness in the right, as God gives us to see the right, let us strive on to finish the work we are in, to bind up the nation's wounds, to care for him who shall have borne the battle and for his widow and his orphans, to do all which may achieve and cherish a just and lasting peace among ourselves and with all nations.[5]

The nation's wounds. The soldiers who have borne the battle. The widows of war. The orphans of war. Gettysburg. Vietnam. Guadalcanal. Iraq. Afghanistan. A dark and empty football field.

"The beginning of the end of war lies in remembrance."

One woman's remembrance was a tiny Matchbox car. My remembrance of the war I fought is a shadow box. I placed it in our home, first above the piano where Kari and Laura practiced and then in my study. Sure, my dad hadn't been a hero when it came to blessing any of us. But honoring his service isn't a lie. It's given us a real way of honoring something about him that is worth honoring. And it has helped me make peace, the best I can, with my past.

• • •

If your story is more like mine (Kari's), meaning that it's not a parent who has caused your blessing wounds, I still encourage you to find some type of "shadow box" to remind you of the decision you've made to forgive the person.

While I don't feel the same need to honor my ex-husband as my father does with his father, being able to forgive him and subsequently bless him were critical to my healing. Because of boundaries I set, I didn't do any of this in conjunction with him. All this was done between the Lord and me. And blessing my ex-husband didn't look anything like breaking boundaries, going back to him, or exhibiting codependence, even in my prayer life. Instead, it looked like reaching a place of forgiveness where, when the negative thoughts and reminders would come into my mind, I could look at them and say, *No. I forgive him. Lord, I choose to bless him. And I'm walking in Your truth, not in lies and hurt.*

Again, we are in no way asking you to break boundaries, falsely treat harmful attributes as positive, or glorify someone who caused you harm. What we *are* asking you to do is to walk through the powerful, biblical, life-changing gift of forgiveness. That's what can take you from war inside you to a peace so deep that you'll be able to feel the freedom of the words *I forgive him (or her). And I bless him (or her).*

"But when we cried out to the LORD, He heard our voice and sent an angel."

NUMBERS 20:16

CHAPTER 18

FINDING EVEN ONE ANGEL TO HELP HOLD UP YOUR ARMS

We're onto the third small step that has helped us and will help you move on from missing the Blessing. It's a step I (John) clearly saw at the same time I saw an angel.

Seeing an angel wasn't an out-of-body experience. It was at the end of an amazing week our family spent across the border from San Diego in blistering hot Tijuana, Mexico. The week before, our whole family had spent seven days at a dude and guest ranch in the beautiful Collegiate Peaks of the Colorado Rockies. I'd been asked to speak at a physicians' retreat.

The sponsors had gone all out to make it a truly five-star experience for the guests. A renowned chef had been flown in. There were daily rides with horses that seemed as well-mannered as the always-attentive wranglers and staff. A river nearby was filled with trout who apparently had gotten the message that they needed to bite for the special guests. And there were wonderful people, including one physician family we got very close to and shared almost every meal with. They even asked if one of our girls could stay for another week to hang out with their daughter, the two of them having become the best of friends.

(I won't say *which* daughter tried to demand to stay there in Colorado, but it was someone who thought another week of five-star camping would be more beneficial than sleeping on rocky ground in old tents for a week, taking baths from buckets, and working all day, dawn to dusk, in Tijuana. But her name might start with *K* and end with *ari*.)

The whole family did, however, fly from Colorado to California. There we met almost eighty other families who had flown in from different parts of the country. Most of them brought tools and experience in building. I was the evening speaker, which is something I could do. (In terms of the building part, I was definitely unskilled labor.)

The first morning, we crawled out of our tents and staggered over to our one-star breakfast prepared by the camp cook, and all the families were divided into teams. Roughly twenty families went to work at each of the four small lots we were assigned to in the barrios.

Picture a small dirt lot scraped clean down to small rocks and gravel. Each team would start from scratch, and in a week, we'd go from digging and pouring the foundation to putting up the walls and roof to installing windows and doors to finishing by stuccoing the entire house.

We'd been told we were building a house for a family who had next to nothing. In our case, we knew that to be true. When we got there, the precious family of five was living in the back of the lot in a cardboard shack.

I'll fast-forward through the amazing amount of work our teams did all week. Each team had some experienced builders who directed everything. But most of what was needed was what people like me could do—manual labor. Some folks ran a vacation Bible school while we were there, but the rest of us used our hands and arms. There were no power tools because there was no electricity.

That meant digging out the foundation by hand and then mixing and pouring the concrete by hand. And on it would go all week. All hand tools and blood, sweat, and tears. A herculean effort by everyone and each team. And for our team, finishing came down to the last day.

Our group of families was down some workers due to several members of our team having drunk unclean water. Unfortunately, these were a few of the bigger guys, who could have made a real difference as we raced to finish.

It was stucco day. And if you've never put stucco on a house: It's a chore. For us, it meant mixing the concrete by hand and then carrying the concrete mix, called mud, to the wall and covering and texturing it from top to bottom with a trowel. It was hard, heavy work, and time was slipping away.

All four groups had a zero-tolerance deadline to get everything finished for their houses on this last day. It was simply too danger-ous to be in the barrio when it was dark. So, starting at the crack of dawn, we had attacked the house, trying to finish the stucco and close many other loops.

Kids were helping mix and carry the cement. Cindy, being a trouper, worked alongside me, doing her best to be like her father, who had stuccoed swimming pools. But we were down quite a few people. And by late afternoon, I knew we weren't going to make it.

We'd be leaving this precious family we were trying to help with an unfinished home. And my arms were giving out. I wouldn't quit, but I was working harder and slower with the last of my strength.

And then it happened.

Suddenly, there was an angel standing right next to me.

One moment I was ready to drop to the ground and admit we'd failed. Then, in what seemed like the next second, someone suddenly stood beside me. An angel.

Actually, the angel was a college-aged young man, throwing stucco up like he was spreading papier-mâché. I realized I'd met him at one of the meals. He and his whole family, in fact, were working alongside me. They had been on a different team. And that's when I realized there were a number of angels running up to the walls to help.

All the other teams had finished their houses. They had heard we were in trouble and were desperate for help, so scores of them had run down the dirt road to our site to help us. Not only did we finish the stucco that day, but we finished every detail of the house. And that whole huge group of families had the unforgettable, eye-watering privilege of surrounding the Mexican family and praying over them and their new house. Of watching as the mission directors handed them the keys to their first real, new, fully stuccoed home.

Suddenly, there was an angel standing right next to me.

We jumped on the bus (I crawled on) and drove back across the border. From there, we said goodbye to the many families going directly to the airport. For Cindy, Kari, Laura, and me, it was time to go to a nice hotel for our first real baths in a week. Dinner at a real restaurant tasted like a ten-star meal. A night in real beds before we headed home the next day was wonderful. And the next morning, over a really great breakfast, everyone—*especially Kari*—agreed that this week had been far better than any five-star guest-ranch retreat could ever be.

The People You Need to Hold Up Your Arms

There was no strength left in my arms the moment before those blessed angels showed up. But while I can't explain it, once the reinforcements came, I wasn't even tired. That's why the next thing we want you to pray about and do is to find some angels around you. *Even one angel is fine.* It should be someone who can encourage you as you take these steps toward building attachment and blessing with others over the next days and weeks.

This shouldn't be a one-sided relationship. Find someone who can help you and whom you can also help with whatever challenges he or she is facing.

Even if you just moved to a new state and city and haven't unpacked, much less found a new church or new friends, you can do this. It only takes one. And, if necessary, it can be a friend from the place you left—someone you can talk with for a few minutes a week on FaceTime after the kids go down.

We can't encourage you enough to do this. Find someone to come alongside you and your family as you seek to move past missing the Blessing.

In Exodus 17, a great battle takes place. God's people fight the Amalekites. As long as Moses holds up his rod, the Israelites are winning. But Moses' arms grow tired, and when he lowers them, the tide of battle turns.

To his rescue come two friends who must seem to Moses like angels. As Aaron and Hur see him struggling to keep his arms up, they come and stand on each side of him and hold up his arms.

For many of us who have missed the Blessing, friend building may not be our strongest gift. It's common for us to struggle with making friends outside our families. But along with all the other emotional, physical, and spiritual changes you can begin to make in Christ now as a person of blessing, it's important to take the first steps toward relational changes. Start recruiting some angels (you need them!)—and start being the kind of supportive angel friend someone else needs as well.

Here's a suggestion that might help.

Host a Dinner for Eight Night

Cindy came up with this idea when we had just moved to Texas and were angel-less. There were lots of young couples in our church. But—like looking at fish who won't bite—how can you catch someone long enough to make friends? There didn't seem to be enough time to meet people in the parking lot after church or during the two minutes they told everyone to stand up and turn and meet someone new.

So Cindy started something she called Dinner for Eight.

She found one couple and asked them to find one other couple—who would also ask another couple—to all join us for dinner one night. It wasn't a forever commitment, just Dinner for Eight one time.

The four couples had a great time getting acquainted. And in the end, everyone agreed this Dinner for Eight thing would be great to do once a month. We were all young and broke. So this meant meeting at someone's house for a potluck or meeting at a food court with lots of low-cost options. Today, almost nothing is low cost, but Coffee for Eight or Yogurt for Eight will work too. It's a great way to build relationships.

If you're single, you could find one person who will find another person who will find one more and make it a Dinner for Four. Just take the bold step to reach out to that first person. You never know—he or she just might become an angel in your life.

In our church, several other couples wanted in on our group, so we had them do their own Dinners for Eight. Then another set of four couples made a group. Before you knew it, we got the church's blessing to start a couples' class! And guess what we made everyone new to the class do? Meet with other new couples in a Dinner for Eight.

We need other people.

And know this: *The wolf loves lone sheep.*

Be an Angel Yourself

In moving past missing the Blessing, we need those angel-like friends who can help us keep our arms up and live out the Blessing. But what can also really help is something I (John) saw Kari model in high school, and that's for *you* to be someone else's angel.

Her freshman year in high school, Kari, along with five other freshmen and one sophomore, had surprised themselves and everyone else by winning the Arizona state cheerleading competition for small schools. Those seven girls were the only ones who had tried out for the team.

Then came her sophomore year, and forty girls tried out!

This time, twelve girls were chosen to be on the varsity cheer squad. They were outstanding, and they, too, won state. But what touched my heart was what Kari did with the last girl chosen that year.

Her name was Brooke. She was a senior, and she was different from the other girls on the squad. She didn't lack heart, spirit, a smile, or enthusiasm. But she was the only one with cerebral palsy and confined to an electric wheelchair.

In most cases, you can only dream of being a cheerleader if you can't walk, you struggle to speak, and you can't do jumps or stunts. But in Brooke's case, the whole squad and their cheer coach, Mrs. Lester, voted her onto the team.

I remember the first football game that year. We live in Arizona. It's *hot* in September, even at seven o'clock in the evening, when the game kicked off. Picture two rows of cheerleaders in their sharp white outfits laced with red and blue, their school colors. Kari stood next to Brooke on the far right side in the front row. You could tell that Kari was proud to be next to her friend.

She didn't lack heart, spirit, a smile, or enthusiasm. But she was the only one with cerebral palsy and confined to an electric wheelchair.

When the girls turned to face the field with their hands on their hips, Brooke moved the toggle on her wheelchair to face the field with them. When they turned back toward the crowd to do a cheer, Brooke turned with them, her arms and voice in sync.

I didn't see much of the game because I couldn't take my

eyes off Kari and Brooke. I was staggered by the courage Brooke showed in struggling to do each cheer the best she could. I was floored by the way Kari would pick up Brooke's pom-poms when she dropped them or make sure Brooke was getting enough to drink from her water bottle.

Yes, others on the cheer squad did a great job of affirming Brooke too. But how many high school cheerleaders would have the courage, love, and willingness to drop the façade of being perfect or "too cool" to be bothered by someone different from the rest?

When their team lost its first game of the season, there was Kari hugging Brooke. Walking alongside her. Being an angel and blessing her friend.

Look, then, for a person who might be harder to bless or even more in need of your blessing than most. And if God shows such a person to you, then picking up her pom-poms or getting him a drink on a hot night can do wonders in moving you past missing the Blessing. Get your eyes off what you missed and on what someone else needs, and find great joy as Jesus cheers you on.

Worry does not empty tomorrow of its sorrow,
it empties today of its strength.

CORRIE TEN BOOM, *Clippings from My Notebook*

CHAPTER 19

SO KEEP
LOOKING DOWN!

As you begin moving past missing the Blessing, it's fair to say that the first three things we've encouraged you to do are small, if not easy: reading pictures of blessing in Scripture, picking a day when your war ends and creating your own "shadow box," and having the courage to reach out and find *that one friend* (at the same time seeking to be an "angel" who helps hold up others' arms).

Now we come to a step that's not only small but super small. Just lower your head and drop your eyes. In other words, *just keep looking down.*

We know you're used to being asked to *look up.* There's even that wonderful verse in the Psalms: "I will raise my eyes to the mountains; from where will my help come?" (Psalm 121:1).

But we're asking you to *keep looking down.* So how is this any way to take a small step in moving away from missing the Blessing?

The View from "Heavenly Places"

The Bible refers to "heavenly places" five times, and it provides a tremendous promise that is linked to the Blessing. Interestingly, those two words are found in Scripture only five times, all in the book of Ephesians.

In the heavenly places, we'll find every spiritual blessing.

The first time *heavenly places* shows up is in Ephesians 1:3: "Blessed be the God and Father of our Lord Jesus Christ, who has *blessed us with every spiritual blessing* in the *heavenly places* in Christ" (emphasis added).

Hold on to that promise for a moment. Wherever the heavenly places are, one thing we know is that we get a blessing when we get there. In fact, we're surrounded by the Blessing. Jesus has blessed us such that *every spiritual blessing* surrounds us.

You and I may have missed the Blessing here on earth. But we can't miss it in the heavenly places with Jesus. In fact, *blessing seems to be the very culture these places are filled with.* The air we breathe. *But where are these places?*

The heavenly places are at the Father's right hand.

The second use of *heavenly places* is in Ephesians 1:20. There we read, ". . . which He brought about in Christ, when He raised Him from the dead and seated Him at His right hand in the heavenly places."

So that's where the heavenly places are! Where Jesus, after His death, resurrection, and ascension, is seated. He's in a place of honor—at God the Father's right hand.

But now it gets even better and more amazing!

Guess who gets to sit at Jesus' right hand—right now!

In Ephesians 2:6, we find the third time *heavenly places* is used. Here we're told something even more amazing: "[God] raised us up with Him, and seated us with Him in the heavenly places in Christ Jesus."

This is where it gets mind-boggling. We know, even if we've

only been to Sunday school a few times, that Jesus has gone up to heaven. That's what is said in the previous verse. But this verse is saying something very different. Take a look at it again:

"[God the Father] raised us up with [Jesus], and seated [you and me] with Him in the heavenly places in Christ Jesus."

So—amazingly, incredibly, lovingly—guess where you're sitting *right now*?

If I (John) were to answer that question, I'd say, "I'm sitting right here in Arizona." But that's not all there is to it. I'm sitting in Arizona, but at the same time, I'm also sitting next to Jesus in the heavenly places.

If Kari were to answer that question, she'd say, based on this verse, "I'm in Washington state . . . *and* I'm sitting next to Jesus right now."

Wherever you are, you're sitting or standing or jogging or in your car right where you are, but you're also in the heavenly places, where Jesus is! That's a reserved-seating place of honor. Of significance. This is true of us because in Christ we are blessed in every way possible!

I'm sitting in Arizona, but at the same time, I'm also sitting next to Jesus in the heavenly places.

Again, you may have missed every element of the Blessing. You may be from a home that withheld the Blessing. But that's not where you are today if you're in Christ!

From the heavenly places, you're *looking down* on all the challenges you're facing. You're seated next to someone (Jesus), so you're never alone in facing them. You're surrounded with every spiritual blessing, so if you're struggling to have even the basics where you're seated on earth, your cup of life from sitting in the heavenly places can be full to overflowing!

Now you can see why it's a powerful small step, if you're serious about moving past missing the Blessing, to realize where you're sitting right now and *keep looking down!*

So Keep Looking Down!

Now let's go back to that idea of the heavenly places. This phrase is also translated "heavenly realms." On the day you came to know Jesus as your Lord and Savior, you entered a new realm. You passed the sign with a cross and moved into another country. Another jurisdiction. Another place. Again, amazingly, you're sitting right now next to Jesus. And you have all the spiritual blessings right now!

Immediate, direct access to Jesus right now. That's way better than a backstage pass. You're right there next to our Lord and Savior!

In Christ, you're now invited to sit down with Him. To hang out. To be right next to Him in the heavenly places. It started with that past event the moment you came to know Him, like me that night at the Kachina Theatre in Scottsdale, Arizona. But from that moment on, I have been seated with Him. I'm seated with Him right now, and I will be seated with Him in the future as well. If you're His child by faith, that's true of you, too.

And here's one last thing that's incredibly helpful. It has to do with the final time *heavenly places* comes up in Ephesians, found in Ephesians 6:12. That's where Paul makes it clear that in this present world there's a spiritual dimension to our lives. This reality goes far beyond the physical.

"For our struggle," we're told, "is not against flesh and blood, but against the rulers, against the powers . . . against the spiritual forces of wickedness in the heavenly places."

This is a tough world filled with many big problems. We will face major challenges and even evil in this world. But we do *not* have to face any of it alone.

You may have missed the Blessing, with all the negative implications that come with that. But that's not all there is to life! Right now, you're seated next to Jesus. All the challenges you are facing are real, be they financial, personal, physical, emotional, or spiritual. But you're not doing life alone.

This can give you a far different perspective when life gets tough, a far different understanding of who you are! Of who you can become when you come to know and be fully and forever attached to Jesus. You're safe. Secure. No matter what.

Right now, you can look at life through God's promises, not just through your problems!

You can wake up from the bad dream of a hurtful past. You can make a new choice to bless instead of curse. To choose life over death, no matter what has happened in the past.

And when you do, know that even neurologically, God has created you with something called neuroplasticity. That's a fancy name for the reality that you really can change. You can reroute and rewire your brain and launch new neural pathways in how you look at and do life.

Right now, you can look at life through God's promises, not just through your problems!

That's the secret strength my mother had and that all of us in Christ can have as well.

The Secret Strength My Mother Had

She should have been bitter and broken and frozen inside. She had every reason to be. Her father had chosen to spend her childhood years far away from his family as he'd tried and failed to keep a dying farm from sinking into the Dust Bowl.

Years later, after only one year of marriage, her first husband had walked into the big sun parlor of their home in Indiana and announced that their relationship was over. There was another woman.

After that dark afternoon, there came a move to Phoenix to see the sun again. It was a new start, and a few years after arriving there, a new marriage. Then the long-awaited birth of children: three boys in just three years.

But just when she might have thought life was getting good, there came a replay of the conversation in the Indiana sun parlor. Another husband (my father) came home to say there was another woman and he was leaving. There would be no further discussion, and in the future, no financial help or even cards or visits with us boys as we grew up.

The three most significant men in my mother's life all walked away from her. The two husbands didn't merely leave but underscored their sudden departures by choosing others over her.

She could have grown full of anger, hurt, shame, and self-pity. She might have looked down at herself and her circumstances in despair and rejection. But instead, she remained vibrant and alive, warm and loving.

Which always amazed me. It doesn't usually happen that way. Author Gerald Sittser writes, "We live life as if it were a motion picture. Loss turns life into a snapshot. The movement stops; everything freezes."[1]

That's what Kari and I have seen over the years in the lives of many people we've counseled and coached. People who have suffered great loss often become people shrink-wrapped and shelved or turned to stone inside.

It should have happened to her. She should have shut down and closed the book on growth and creativity and connection—if not for the relational losses she suffered, then certainly for all the physical losses that added injury to insult. Rheumatoid arthritis would twist her hands, tear up her knees, and take away an outstanding career. It would take, too, any realistic chance of remarrying. As her bones dried up, her spirit should have also dried up and cracked and broken. She should have given up.

Particularly on me.

I was the one who was asked to leave grade school for a stupid mistake. I was the one the police carried home late one night. I was the one who brought home report cards so dismal they wouldn't even qualify me to ask, "Paper or plastic?"

Yet my mom never gave up on life, learning, friends, the parade of struggling people the Lord brought into her life . . . or her sons. Without a doubt, she was one of the most loving people I've ever known. Even in her last days, she "glowed" (a description given to me by one of her hospice nurses).

But why? What enabled her to carry on? What gave her the strength to continue? How could she do it?

After a night of crying out in pain from the arthritis each time she rolled over in bed, she could still greet us with a genuine smile in the morning. For years I wondered how. And what was it that allowed her to look beyond her own pain and loss and "adopt" hurting kids the way other people bring home stray cats? What was it that kept her mind alert and her arthritic fingers still tapping across her computer keyboard? (She was on the internet before I was!) Why didn't she daily stir up her regrets and hurts, put down my father in front of us, or take the counsel of Job's wife and turn and curse God (see Job 2)?

What was her secret?

Today I realize she really did have a secret, the same one I've been advocating in this chapter. Mom really did believe with all her heart that Jesus was sitting right next to her in life, and she next to Him.

That's how she chose to live, as if Jesus really were right there with her. She was looking down on all those trials and losses in a different way, from a different vantage point. From the heavenly places.

I know that in getting the Blessing from Jesus in many ways (every way), she committed to giving it to people around her as long as she had breath and life. She started with us boys, but she reached many others whom she touched. She was so broken she couldn't offer physical labor to help. But she was a Jedi Knight when it came to giving reparative therapy to others who were hurting emotionally and spiritually. She helped them know that Jesus was with them, even in the toughest times. She helped them see life from a different perspective. And these are things we, too, can do as we become people of blessing.

So that's the fourth small step we'd ask you to consider as you move past missing the Blessing: *to know who you really are.*

To realize where you're seated *right now.*

Yes, the problems and challenges, both past and present, are real and can be hugely hurtful. People and spiritual forces are negative and very real. But you are *not* alone. You don't have to stay stuck in a life without blessing. You can, in Jesus, swim in every spiritual blessing.

So in summary . . .

Keep looking down.

Keep believing that Jesus is sitting in the heavenly places and that you're right there with Him today and every day.

Keep holding on to His promises, not your problems.

We have a friend who often says, *"You can't hold anger and love in the same hand. You can't hold hate and joy in the same hand."*

But you can reach out and hold His hand whom you're seated next to right now in the heavenly places. You can drop whatever you're holding on to that has ruined and threatens to continue to ruin your life. You can reach out and find that Jesus reaches back. You can be in Phoenix, Tacoma, Tulsa, New York, Texas, or California and still be in the heavenly places, surrounded with every spiritual blessing, looking down on a landscape that doesn't have to discourage or destroy you.

God's blessing can help you hold on to the ultimate, not just struggle with the chaos and uncertainty of the immediate.

Through a lens of navigation, then, we can see that "keeping" isn't about having a perfect, linear, or flawless journey; keeping is about having a focus point *that you want to keep* moving toward.

BENJAMIN L. COREY, *Unafraid: Moving beyond Fear-Based Faith*

CHAPTER 20

HOW GOD'S *BEING THERE* CAN HELP YOU BUILD LOVING ATTACHMENT

We've so far looked at several small but significant steps we can take to move past missing the Blessing. This next one consists of just two words that can help you bless others with loving attachment.

As God promised, you can *be there*.

These two words are at the heart of God's love for you. They're also at the heart of what attachment science shows to be essential in making a choice to move away from hurt and start loving and blessing others.

The Bible verse that captures this concept is 2 Chronicles 7:16: "I have chosen and consecrated [the Temple] so that My name may be there forever, and My eyes and My heart will be there always."

Did you note the two times you read the words *be there*? Note also the four words that explain what they mean: God will be there *forever* for us with His *name* on us, His *eyes* looking for our best, and a *heart* that matches and values our emotions.

Grab hold of this simple verse, and you're well on your way to being an attachment expert. According to the researchers—but even more important, according to the One who created bonding and attachment—these words picture four ways of "being there" that are key to attachment. Let's start with the experts.

To take one example, Sue Johnson was a champion for research into connection, attachment, and caring for couples. She developed the celebrated marriage and family therapy called Emotionally Focused Therapy (EFT). In her outstanding book *Created for Connection*, Sue and her coauthor, Kenny Sanderfer, lay out the basics of her therapy in a take-home, layman-ready way. And as Sue and Kenny and the Bible say, love is not a bargain but an unshakable bond![1]

When we build attachment, we bless people physically, emotionally, mentally, and spiritually. We build that kind of security and blessing into someone's life when we answer three attachment questions used in EFT.[2] (Note that these are based on hundreds of research studies.)

1. When I reach out, will you reach back? Do you see my needs, and will you step toward me?
2. Am I enough? Do you really see high value in me?
3. Will you stay with me? Even in the tough times, will you stay committed to me?

EFT therapists ask couples who are struggling to build or maintain loving bonds to grapple with these questions. Can you see, from what we've learned, how the Blessing helps answer all three? Even more, how Scripture can boil down attachment to just the two words *be there*?

Almighty God promised His people He would be there for them. And we can live out God's love and be there for the people in our lives when we learn to bless as well.

Let's go back to that verse God gave to Solomon in 2 Chronicles.

If we were to write it out word by word as it reads in Hebrew, here's the order of words and how it would look:

will be My *name* there
forever
and will be My **eyes** and My **heart** there
always

Almighty God woke Solomon in the middle of the night to give him this promise. (If you really want to grab someone's attention, call him at three in the morning.) It's a promise that answers each of the three attachment questions. Let's see how it can help you move toward becoming a person of blessing.

"Forever My Name Will Be There"

It all starts with forever.

The core of attachment science is the fact that we are built for relationship and connection and suffer physically when that attachment is withdrawn. We long for someone to be there instead of walk away or ignore us. It's at the core of each person's being to need someone to reach back when we reach out.

It's at the core of each person's being to need someone to reach back when we reach out.

For those of us who missed the Blessing, that's a picture we didn't have. But it's absolutely the picture of a loving God. Noted author Henri Nouwen puts it this way:

God loved you before you were born, and God will love you after you die. In Scripture, God says, "I have loved you with an everlasting love." This is a very fundamental truth of your identity. This is who you are whether you feel it or not. You belong to God from eternity to eternity. Life is just a little opportunity for you during a few years to say, "I love you, too."[3]

Max Lucado, with his world-class devotional skills, boils it down to this:

> If God had a refrigerator, your picture would be on it.
> If He had a wallet, your photo would be in it. He sends
> you flowers every spring and a sunrise every morning. . . .
> Face it, friend. He is crazy about you!⁴

That's what we've been telling you throughout this book! It's what changed my (Kari's) life when God showed up for me in that dark apartment. It's what changed my dad's life as a teenager on the night he realized Jesus wasn't going anywhere. It's what loving parents, grandparents, aunts, and uncles do when they say and show to a child of any age, *"I'm not going anywhere. I'll be there in the tough times and in the good times."*

That doesn't mean we have to live out the Blessing perfectly. Trying to be there perfectly for someone is actually a great way to rob the person of the Blessing. Pursuing perfection means you're always walking on ice, focused on not falling and unable to enjoy the relationship. Accept the fact that occasionally, even as you remain committed to rebuilding broken bonds, you'll mess up.

You're doing well when you provide predictable blessing to others—when your child doesn't have to go to the neighbors or Disneyland to find joy, love, and attachment. It's there in your home. And how do you do that? By having your name, your eyes, and your heart *be there* consistently.

God's name will be there for you.

Like almighty God telling Solomon three ways He was committed to being there for His people, we can bless others and build attachment with *our names*, *our eyes*, and *our hearts*. But is a name really that important? After all, parents give children names all the time that suggest the person making the choice was under the influence. (Anyone for naming a child Ima Hogg or Moon Unit?)

Parents today usually look outside their child when picking his or her name. Often a name is a way to honor a favorite relative, sports hero, or entertainer. But in biblical times, a person's name stood for who he or she was on the inside. That's why you see Jesus giving His disciple Simon a new name when He looked at him and saw something more there. Simon became Peter (the "rock"). Jesus changed his name because of who he could become.

In the book of Proverbs, we're told, "A good name is to be more desired than great wealth" (Proverbs 22:1). We even get a new name when we get to heaven (see Revelation 22:3-4) given to us by God!

We read in 2 Chronicles about how Solomon was told that God's name would be there with him and his people. It was like saying, "You all have just made the team. You get to wear the jersey with the team's name and logo on it."

But is having someone choose to put his or her name on you really that important? I (John) told you earlier how much it meant to me when I accidentally met my Uncle Max. He was the one who told me a lot about my father's past. Max became, in many ways, the father I'd never had.

Years after we'd first met at the SMU library, I had married and moved back to Arizona. Sadly, Aunt Sally had passed, and Uncle Max was still living in Dallas. It was then that I got a letter from him, handwritten in black ink. I still have it. In fact, it's folded up and in the backpack that's a few feet from me.

Dear John,

It may come as a surprise to learn that I have been discussing a living will. However, I am sure that you will agree with the principle. I hope the time will never come when you have to execute it, but when it does, I know you will do it well.

In short, my Uncle Max was dying. He was asking me to make sure there were no medical heroics. To follow the directions his lawyer would send me about what to do when all that could be done had been done.

But then, at the end of the letter, he wrote something I cherish. In fact, if you run into me at the airport someday and I'm carrying my backpack, feel free to ask to see the letter. I carry it with me everywhere. The letter ends with these words—and Uncle Max putting his name on me:

Thank you, John.
You have helped me so much in the past, and I am sure you will continue to do so—because you are my son.

Affectionately,
Max

I carry my father's name. But he never chose to put it on me. He never chose to bless me, to claim me, to be there for me. But Uncle Max did. I have his name on it. In writing. *I am his son.*

So *know first and foremost that God has put His name on you.* You made His team because of His love. And there's no being cut or traded if you lose a step, lose your hair, or lose your teeth. His name stays on you forever, even in heaven.

Know first and foremost that God has put His name on you.

And from that unshakable base of attachment, you can now reach out in love to those around you, as my Uncle Max did for me. Tell them they have *your name.* Your love. That they're chosen and unconditionally accepted, even if they make some errors or drop a few balls. They're on your team. Whether they get your name legally, like with your own child, or by your choice, like Uncle Max with me, it's an incredibly powerful way to bless.

God's eyes are on you always.

Our eyes are important in providing appropriate, meaningful touch. To look at someone with joy on your face expresses love and attachment and conveys the Blessing powerfully.

We're told, "For the eyes of the LORD roam throughout the earth, so that He may strongly support those whose heart is completely His" (2 Chronicles 16:9). God delights in taking advantage of ways He can support us—ways He can be there for us and bless us.

Now it's time for you to use your eyes to become a student of those you want to bless. Don't look critically, seeing all their faults. Look with discernment on who God has gifted them to be, what strengths and potential they have that you can point out. Say things like "Wow! You are so sensitive in picking up on the needs of others. I wouldn't be surprised if God used that sensitivity to help lots of people when you grow up."

Or you might say, "You are so determined! I'll bet the Lord uses that awesome spirit of determination to solve problems and help do important things in people's lives."

If you see it, say it, even if what you're seeing is just a potential strength for now. In doing so, you're *being there*, pointing out the person's value and letting him or her know that, as far as your eyes can see, he or she is more than enough.

God's heart will be there.

Let's return to another of those three important attachment questions: *When I reach out, will you reach back?*

That's the appropriate, meaningful touch aspect of reaching out and reaching back. But for attachment scientists (and EFT therapists) and in Scripture, reaching out is more than just physical touch. It's having a heart that responds and links with someone else's heart, that acknowledges or identifies with a loved one's emotions!

When someone reaches out, hoping for someone to reach back, he or she is expressing *an emotional need as well as a physical one.* There's a need behind the deed.

I reach out because I'm lonely. Tired. Hurting. Sad. Scared. Will you reach back? And when you do, it's you seeing, valuing, validating, attuning, and blessing my emotional need. You're not uncomfortable with my emotions or demanding that I "quit being so emotional and make sense!"

Someone reaching out is asking, "Will you reach back in a way that emotionally connects with me?"

What an amazing thing to know that Jesus, the Lord of lords Himself, cares about where we are *emotionally*! Jesus shared our emotions. He cried at the death of a friend. Rejoiced at a wedding ceremony. Got angry at those desecrating God's house. Showed compassion to a hemorrhaging woman's small touch. Saw and stepped toward a woman whose anguish in losing her only son moved Him—so much that He raised up her son from the dead and gave him back to her!

Jesus is able to come alongside and sit with us if we're scared. He can be there for us, cheering us on when we get something right, like when Peter correctly identified who He was. Forgiving us when we fall short, as He also did with Peter. Redeeming and restoring us so we can heal. Lifting us up when we need something more than "Just suck it up."

This is why it's important that, as we begin to live out the Blessing, we embrace and don't ignore the emotional side of life. A lot of emotion is seen in all the times the Blessing is given in Scripture. Emotions are a huge part of blessing others by attaching to them!

In contrast, choosing not to seek to understand someone's emotional needs is a relationship killer. For example, have you ever said to someone, or had someone say to you, "My heart's just not in it."

That's what it feels like when we miss the Blessing. We know that a significant person should have loved us, should have built that bond with us, *but his heart just wasn't in it.* She never sought or chose to emotionally connect with us.

We love *The Living Bible*'s paraphrase of Psalm 139:17-18. It's a song of David written at a time when he was hurting, alone, and being hunted. It shows how God's heart is there for us always.

> How precious it is, Lord, to realize that you are thinking
> about me constantly! I can't even count how many times
> a day your thoughts turn toward me. And when I waken
> in the morning, you are still thinking of me!

That's a picture of attuning to someone's heart—of sharing his heart! May we likewise *be there* for those we seek to bless by turning toward them, reaching back when they reach out emotionally.

To move past missing the Blessing, then, let's embrace these four ways of being there for others in imitation of our Lord:

- "I'll love you forever."
- "You carry my name with you."
- "My eyes see how God has gifted you."
- "My heart goes out to what you're feeling and dealing with."

"Nobody knows the trouble I've seen" goes the old spiritual, and of course nobody knows the trouble we have any of us seen—the hurt, the sadness, the bad mistakes, the crippling losses—but we know it. We are to remember it. And the happiness we have seen too—the precious times, the precious people . . .

FREDERICK BUECHNER,
A Room Called Remember: Uncollected Pieces

Hey . . . Dad . . . you wanna have a catch?

RAY KINSELLA, *Field of Dreams*

CHAPTER 21

PREPARING FOR THE DAY THE DREAM OF A BLESSING ENDS

We started this book with a reference to the movie *Field of Dreams*.[1] Let's take another look at it.

Ray Kinsella builds a ballpark in his Iowa cornfield in response to a mysterious voice saying, "If you build it, he will come."

Other messages come to Ray just as mysteriously.

"Ease his pain."

"Go the distance."

Ray becomes obsessed with trying to solve the meaning of these cryptic messages. Piece by piece, the puzzle comes together. When the ballplayers from the 1919 White Sox team show up, Ray assumes the voices he's heard referred to their star player, Shoeless Joe Jackson. But what Ray discovers in the final scene is that the one who needed to come, whom he built the ballpark for, was his father. *"If you build it, he will come."*

And that the pain to be eased was Ray's.

It's the pain of a scandal in baseball. It's the pain of a son who never received his father's blessing. The picture is of a washed-out bridge between a father and his son, of words that were never spoken and words that were never heard.

When the father appears in that final scene, Ray gets a chance to start rebuilding that bridge.

"What do I say to him?" Ray asks his wife, Annie, as he sees his father on the field.

"Why don't you introduce him to his granddaughter?" she says.

Ray's father, John Kinsella, walks up to them.

"Hi. Just wanted to thank you folks for putting up this field and letting us play here. I'm John Kinsella," he says, extending his hand.

"I'm Ray," he says, shaking it.

Ray turns to his daughter to introduce her to his father, but he stumbles over the words. "This is my—this is John."

"Hi, John," says his daughter, Karen.

Ray and John begin to walk together.

"You catch a good game," Ray says to his father.

"Thank you. It's so beautiful here. For me—for me it's like a dream come true. Can I ask you something? *Is this heaven?*"

"It's Iowa."

"Iowa? I could have sworn it was heaven," says John.

"Is there a heaven?"

"Oh yeah," says John. "It's the place dreams come true."

Ray looks around and sees Annie and Karen on the porch. "Maybe this is heaven."

"Goodnight, Ray," his father says.

"Goodnight, John." The two shake hands, and the father walks off. But before he gets away, Ray calls to him, his voice cracking.

"Hey . . . Dad . . . you wanna have a catch?"

And the father says to his long-searching son, "I'd like that."

And the two toss the ball back and forth in casual arcs. As the sun goes down, Annie turns on the field lights. And as the camera lifts toward the horizon, we see a winding road of cars with their headlights on, all coming to see this field of dreams.

What a wonderful ending scene! How much like the ending I

(John) dreamed about with my father! I longed for some kind of scene with my own dad where we had the chance to speak such words, hear such words—a chance, finally, after all those years, to ease my pain.

The Day I Almost Heard a Blessing

It was a beautiful spring day. I was at work when my office manager came running to my desk. "You need to get on the phone," she said. "It's the hospital!"

It turned out my father, who was living on his own at the time, had just had a heart attack *and had driven himself to the hospital.* He collapsed on his way into the emergency ward, which sounds like an old Marine. The hospital staff had been trying to locate some next of kin. In his wallet, they had found my business card, which I had given him several years before.

I called my older brother, Joe (Jeff was out of state), and from different parts of the city, we raced to St. Luke's Hospital. When we arrived, the woman behind the reception desk said, "Oh! You're the ones I'm supposed to take to the surgeon."

She walked Joe and me back through the maze of rooms and medical equipment to a small office. The doctor, in green scrubs, looked up and confirmed we were Joe Trent's boys.

"I wanted to talk to you before we took your father into surgery," he said. "You know he's in terrible shape physically, right?"

We knew. He was a chain-smoker, was an alcoholic, and during the war had contracted malaria that still flared up.

"I want you to know I'm going to do all I can for him . . . but . . . I'm not going to lie to you. The odds are we are probably going to lose him on the table. So if there's something you want to say to your father, *this would be a really good time to say it.*"

Say what? Oceans of things had been left unsaid. Now, out of all of them, what could or should I say?

They took us back to where our father was already lying on a large metal table. The IV drip had just been inserted, and he was prepped for surgery. As far as I knew, this would be the last time I'd see him on earth.

We were given three minutes to talk with him.

No magic words came to mind. All I did was go over, pat Dad on the leg, and tell him we loved him, we were praying for him, and we'd be waiting for him when he got out of surgery.

Then he looked up at Joe and me and said, "Well, boys . . ."

There was a long pause.

"I guess I ought to say something."

Then an even longer pause.

We stood by his bedside, waiting. Not a word was spoken until a few minutes later when the nurses came in and wheeled him away. Joe and I were left standing there, alone, as those cold, polished aluminum doors swung shut.

Ever since I'd first met my dad, I'd felt like he had things he wanted to say but somehow couldn't. I kept waiting for those words to come. Hoping. Longing. Aching for those words.

Maybe if he pulled through. Maybe then.

And he did pull through. And then came the last time I could have received his blessing.

It was a Sunday, August 9, and my wife, Cindy, had just finished getting the girls dressed and fixing their hair to go to church. We started down the hall to get in the car when the phone rang. I picked it up.

"Dr. Trent, you'd better come to the hospice right away."

We all gathered in the hallway and prayed for Grandpa. I sent them off to church, and I headed to the hospice . . . and to my one last chance to hear those words, to feel that embrace, to see something in his eyes, his smile—some hint somewhere that he cared, that I mattered, that he loved me, that he was sorry for all the missing years, all the pain—something.

For the next eight hours, I sat holding my father's hand. I listened to his desperate struggle to breathe and watched him slip away, one gasp at a time. I got him water, ice chips, another pillow, a blanket, whatever he needed or wanted. I spoke, but only when he wanted to talk. When the coughing spells got bad, I prayed for him—only to have him cuss me out for pushing Jesus on him. He never said a positive word to me the whole time. No words of love or healing.

At 4:43 in the afternoon, as I held his hand, he breathed his last and died.

And so did something I had longed for all my life.

When the coughing spells got bad, I prayed for him—only to have him cuss me out for pushing Jesus on him.

In the Old Testament, another twin named Esau suddenly realized he would never receive his father's blessing. We're told that "he cried out with an exceedingly great and bitter cry, and said to his father, 'Bless me, me as well, my father!'" (Genesis 27:34).

I knew how Esau felt. The very words he longed to hear from his father I longed to hear from mine.

"Bless me, Father. *Please.* Bless me."

I'd dreamed that he would do that someday. And that someday the two of us would have a catch.

When Your Dream of the Blessing Dies

In this whole section of the book, we've tried to give you small steps to take in stepping away from missing the Blessing. This one is especially tough. Because the day may come—if it hasn't already—when after all your prayers, longing, trying, and perhaps, like me, failing, that person who never chose to bless you passes away. And so, too, any earthly chance to receive the Blessing.

There's an outstanding ministry called GriefShare. About a year after my father passed away, I got a call from them. They were asking me to make a video on not having a happy ending when a loved one passes away. They wanted me to talk about what it was like to lose my father.

In that video, I tried hard to honor my father but to be honest as well. I talked about how hard I had tried to do something my good friend Dr. Gary Rosberg calls "closing the loop." But I couldn't close the loop with my father.

I had written and spoken to more than a million men at Promise Keepers. More than a million more people had read my books about the Blessing. Over the years, I'd heard from hundreds of people and families who had read a book or heard a message and began to reverse the curse. Often I heard stories about how a person who had previously refused to bless finally had. What a celebration!

So I could help others, but I couldn't do the same thing with my own father?

I remember going in to clean and pack up my father's apartment after he died. There at the bottom of a bookcase was the book I had coauthored and given him, *The Blessing*.

I opened the book, thinking maybe he had written some note or thought in it.

It was the first edition, a hardback book. Have you ever opened a hardback for the first time? Heard that creak a stitched book makes when you do?

He'd not only not read it; he'd never even opened it.

Which was just one more picture of our relationship.

But I am grateful for several things I'd done in advance, small things you may want to consider or at least be aware of before that day.

You Can't Out-Logic Emotions

One step you can take if you're losing or just lost a loved one who never blessed you is to realize that you can't out-logic emotions.

Let's say you're at the movie theater. Right when the previews are ending and the theater is at its darkest before the movie starts, someone is coming down your aisle with a huge popcorn and two large drinks. You try scooting in, but the person steps right on your foot. *Ouch!* It's summer, and you have sandals on, but he has regular shoes.

What's your *first* reaction when that happens?

Ouch! That hurts! Pain from your foot moves in milliseconds to the brain.

Then, after the stimulus, right along with the pain comes an emotion—*anger!* Someone has just caused pain, and most often, our response is to get ready for a fight.

But let's say this truly was an accident. In fact, let's say the person who stepped on your foot is already being extremely apologetic. He's saying how sorry he is. It was dark, and he didn't see your foot. Could he go and get you some popcorn to apologize? He's so apologetic, in fact, that you finally exhale and say something you don't really feel, like "It's okay. Stuff like that happens."

> *While you can be as logical as you want, you can't out-logic feelings.*

My point is that you can plan for and pray about and try to mentally picture what your reaction will be when a day of loss or hurt comes, when any chance for an earthly blessing from that person is gone. But while you can be as logical as you want, you can't out-logic feelings. And that's okay. Feelings can move faster than any plans you've made to deal with things in a specific way.

Therefore, it's important to pray ahead of time about what might happen. Do some planning. But know that when it happens, emotions may flood in. It may be that you're angry, hurt, sad, feel nothing, or even have positive feelings like *I'm finally free.*

Give yourself grace. Don't do something dishonoring, like the person I worked with who followed through on his promise that on the day of his father's funeral he would dance on his grave. That kind of dishonoring emotion and action just hardwires your hate and chains you to the person who's gone. "Be angry," we're told, "and yet do not sin" (Ephesians 4:26).

Capture Your Thoughts Before and After

If you've read this far and have read other books I've written or coauthored, you'll know that this is far more personally revealing than any other book I've ever done. In part, that's because writing about missing the Blessing touches so close to home for me. It has been hard and humbling yet helpful to capture some of these thoughts and many of these stories in writing. I'd encourage you to do the same.

This is not to say that you have to write a book about your experience missing the Blessing and now learning to give and live it. But Kari and I would encourage you to get a bound journal (not an online one). *Clinical studies are showing that there's something extremely therapeutic about writing out your thoughts with a pen or pencil.* So even if you have terrible handwriting (like most of us), go old school and capture on paper some of the thoughts and prayers swirling around in your mind.

It may be a first for you to try to capture your words. And if it proves too exhausting, it's okay to finally give up and click Record on your phone app and save your thoughts as an audio file. (Then, if you want, have your word processor listen and type them out.)

Think through not just your stories but also what they meant to you. What can you learn from them? What might God have taught you when they happened? What do you need to do now? And finally . . .

Realize You May Have to Go through This Book a Second Time

If you've been reading through this book and the person who never gave you the Blessing is gone, in time, it may well be good to go back through it again.

It's one thing to read this book while there's hope, however slight, that things can change. As mentioned, I have heard countless stories of how someone read *The Blessing*, gave it to his father or mother, and saw God open welded-shut doors and restore relationships. It's fine to pray for and work toward that, but such blessing and healing are not everyone's story. And much of what you've read in these pages with the hope of healing for you can be even more important if there's no chance of change with someone else. All we've written about blessing and attachment and God's love and healing and reversing the curse are even more important to own and put into your life if the person who didn't bless you is gone.

Six weeks after my father's funeral, I had come in from jogging and was walking down the hall when five-year-old Kari came out of her room. This was unusual for two reasons. First, it was *really* early in the morning, and Kari is our let's-get-up-at-the-crack-of-noon child. Second, instead of wearing her usually cheery smile, she had huge tears rolling down her cheeks. I fell to my knees, hugging her as she sobbed.

"Honey, what's wrong?" I asked.

"Oh, Daddy. I just realized Grandpa's gone."

"I know it's hard," I said, trying to comfort her.

"But Daddy . . . *I never got to hug him.*"

By the time my father died, he hadn't even bothered to learn the name of our second daughter, Laura. He'd never picked up either of the girls. Never hugged them. Never held their hands. Nothing. And now the loss of all that was left behind in a little girl's heart.

I don't know why he never hugged us. Maybe his dad had never hugged him. Maybe it went back for generations. But I knew this: It stopped here. I was going to make sure that before I died my family would know they were loved and blessed.

So how do you make a stand like this? As you'll see in the next chapter, it starts by falling on your knees.

WASHINGTON—Hundreds of thousands of praying, singing and somewhat tearful men blanketed the National Mall on Saturday for a giant service of prayer and atonement organized by the Denver-based evangelical group Promise Keepers. Although there was no official crowd estimate, the six-hour gathering appeared to be one of the largest religious events ever recorded in the United States.

ADRIEL BETTELHEIM, *Denver Post*, Sunday, October 5, 1997

As you think about your life over the past few months and year, where does prayer (and especially your "chief prayers") fit into how you order your day? For days when you have not been able to pray when you preferred to, what has been your strategy for finding a time and place where you can pray with concentration? Would you like to ask God to help you in this area of your life?

C. S. LEWIS

CHAPTER 22

STANDING STARTS
ON YOUR KNEES

It was a picture-perfect day, sunny and warm, with fall colors tinting the foliage. I (John) will never forget it. It was Saturday, October 4, 1997. It was the day *more than a million men* converged on the nation's capital.

I stood on a scaffold twenty feet above the ground observing the event. From there I could see that the crowd stretched from a stage across from the Capitol to the Lincoln Memorial nearly three miles away. They stood there for six hours. It was an awesome sight. The men came from every state, every denomination, every race. They came not to picket or to protest. They came to pray. To ask forgiveness for the past. To make a commitment for the future.

They started out standing.

They stood even taller when every man was asked to get on his knees to pray and a million men knelt down.

They called themselves Promise Keepers. They were men of every age and background who wanted to be good husbands, good fathers, good men. They sought to keep their promises to God and their families.

They realized, like an alcoholic in recovery, that they couldn't do it on their own. That's why they knelt on the grassy National Mall to pray.

The picture brought tears to my eyes as I knelt with them. What a picture! And what a reminder to us today of how important this next small step is as we seek to move from curse to blessing.

This is where it starts. On our knees.

We can't become people of blessing on our own. We need grace to look at the pictures from our pasts. We need grace to understand them, to feel compassion for them. And we need grace upon grace to forgive those who have hurt us.

God gives grace to the humble, the Scriptures tell us. And the place the humble go to receive that grace is on their knees. That's where we need to go not only to process the pictures we're left with but also to produce the pictures we want to leave behind.

But here's my problem, and it may be yours, too. All through the history of faith, great saints and great minds (including C. S. Lewis) have struggled to make prayer of any kind a regular priority. And if you just said amen to struggling with prayer, then know that I said it too.

There seem to be two kinds of people who pray.

Two Sides of the Prayer Coin

For some, prayer is like breathing. These are people like Dr. Bruce Waltke, whom I had the privilege of having as a Bible and Hebrew professor. He was a brilliant scholar who had just left Harvard, where he'd taught ancient Semitics, to come chair the Hebrew department at Dallas Seminary.

Every one of Dr. Waltke's classes was a master class on instruction, whatever the subject. But my first class with him taught me more than I'd ever learned before about prayer.

Up to that point, I had never been in a class where the teacher had opened in prayer. I was about to find out that prayer to start a class was the norm at Dallas. Because this was the first class of the new year and a first-year introductory class, Dr. Waltke began by welcoming us and going through a list of instructions. Then he said, "Let's pray, and then we'll begin class."

Only there was no class—except that master class on prayer.

Dr. Waltke started praying and was still praying an hour and ten minutes later when the class bell sounded. I had never prayed for more than ten minutes straight—more likely five—in my young Christian life. I can still struggle with extended periods of prayer.

But prayer was like breathing to Dr. Waltke. When the bell rang and he looked up, startled, he smiled and apologized for going so long. Then he told us we were dismissed and he'd see us the next class.

He never prayed again for an entire class (even though that was a secret hope of students on test days). But I never forgot that first class. And I wish I was that kind of disappear-into-prayer person. Of course, shorter prayers are good as well, such as the one Jesus prayed on the cross in the agony of being nailed to the tree: "Father, forgive them; for they do not know what they are doing" (Luke 23:34).

This isn't a lesson on the length of our prayers or how easy it is for you or me to pray. Rather, we want you to understand that prayer is where we begin when it comes to moving away from the curse and a missing blessing. You don't have to be like Dr. Waltke (unless that's the kind of person God has gifted you to be). But I do encourage you to be honest about any struggles you have with praying for yourself and for those you want to bless.

Prayer is where we begin when it comes to moving away from the curse and a missing blessing.

C. S. Lewis wrote honestly and humbly about the struggles he had with prayer. The last book Lewis wrote was to someone he calls Malcolm, and it is primarily a book about prayer. He describes the struggle he had with falling asleep while praying.

(Anyone besides us relate?) But he also tells us what helped him make prayer more of a priority. He writes,

> My own plan, when hard pressed, is to seize any time, and place, however unsuitable, in preference to the last waking moment. On a day of travelling—with, perhaps, some ghastly meeting at the end of it—I'd rather pray sitting in a crowded train than put it off till midnight when one reaches a hotel bedroom with aching head and dry throat and one's mind partly in a stupor and partly in a whirl. On other, and slightly less crowded days, a bench in a park, or a back street where one can pace up and down, will do.[1]

At whatever time of day works best for you, we encourage you to get in the regular habit of asking God for help on the days when you feel you're slipping back into hating instead of forgiving. Pray for strength to be alert like Jesus to those reaching out to you, to be aware of who's around you and what's going on with them. Pray for someone to be the kind of friend that we talked about earlier, an angel who can help you (and you him or her). In fact, talk about all the things that are on your heart with your heavenly Father.

If you still need some encouragement, I (Kari) can tell you personally just how much of a difference consistent prayer can make. When I was starting my journey of healing from abuse, I took to heart the verse that tells us to take every thought captive (2 Corinthians 10:5). I began to use prayer as my way to fight the lies and abusive words, memories, and thoughts that would seep into my mind every day.

The second I became conscious of one of those painful words, memories, or thoughts, I would pray. Nothing long. Nothing crazy. But something along the lines of *Lord, silence those lies [or words] in the name of Jesus. Father, You don't see me that way. Your Word says I'm chosen. Wanted. And loved. Replace this lie with Your truth. And help me forgive and bless.*

I did this again and again and again. As often as the thoughts would come, I found myself praying these quick but powerful prayers. It was the first time I could actually feel myself making progress. I could see Satan trying to knock me down, and instead of getting hit, I had a real weapon to use. Prayer was stronger than any lie, memory, or attack he could send my way.

Slowly, things began to change. The lies lost their hold. The words no longer stung. The memories faded and were replaced with God's peace, joy, and blessing. Yes, there were other steps—like those we've described in this book—but the power of prayer allowed me to no longer sit in the darkness of the words and emotions that had broken me. Prayer gave me the power, through the power of Jesus and the Holy Spirit, to join the fight. And it made me feel, for the first time, like I could actually win.

Not only did prayer begin to heal my heart, but it has also become a powerful way of building my faith. I began to keep a journal, which I now call my Blessing Journal. It's full of prayers God has answered for things I have asked Him to do, change, heal, or provide. Many have been answered, and some are still in progress. As of this writing, more than fourteen years of testament after testament of God's faithfulness are recorded.

I prayed I would heal from abuse—answered and still being answered (as anyone who has experienced trauma knows). I prayed I'd find an incredible husband—answered when I met Joey. I prayed for a child for Joey and me when we went through five years of fertility challenges—answered again, with a bonus blessing of a second (miracle) baby. More recently, I prayed for my husband's life to be saved when we were in a horrible, life-changing car accident with our two little boys in the backseat. While we're still waiting on some answered prayers for Joey's full healing, I've seen God work miracle after miracle.

God has been faithful even in the unanswered prayers, when He has shown up with something better or more incredible than I ever could have imagined. He has also taught me things my heart has desperately needed with His kind and gentle no.

All this is to say that prayer doesn't need to be complicated, fancy, or prescriptive. Share your heart with God. Use it to fight the challenges that come your way. And be encouraged by it as a way to build your faith and see God's faithfulness firsthand.

Prayer doesn't need to be complicated, fancy, or prescriptive.

Finally, we want to offer a prayer we've adapted for those of us who missed the Blessing. We hope it encourages you to deal with your pain but also to be open to receiving, giving, and living the Blessing.

You can come back to this prayer as often as you need—on days of celebration or challenge. We took it right out of Psalm 103.

A Prayer from Psalm 103 Paraphrased

Oh my soul, teach me to bless.
From head to toe, Lord, let me first bless Your holy name!
My soul thanks You, Lord, for blessing me in every way!
For calling me to the heavenly places where I get to be with
  You—places of blessing!
With Your blessing surrounding me,
help me, Lord, not to forget a single blessing You've showered
  on me.
Not a single one.
Thank You for the Blessing that comes in Your forgiveness of
  my sins—every one.
Thank You for healing me time after time.
Thank You for healing my body and my heart and my mind so
  often!
Thank You for helping me see that I'm more than what I missed.
Thank You for adding back so much beauty when there were
  only ashes.

*Thank You for giving me the strength to hold to Your promises,
 not just my problems.*
*Thank You, Lord, for Your grace and the gift of redeeming me
 from hell, for I was indeed lost and without hope.*
*For meeting me with so much love when I turned back toward
 Your love.*
*For wrapping me in a robe, giving me a ring, crowning me with
 love and mercy.*
For wrapping me in goodness and helping me see beauty again.
*For restoring my soul and bringing rest where there used to be so
 much chaos.*
Lord, You are the One who can put victims back on their feet.
You put me back on my feet.
You are the One who can create a new plan in my heart,
*who has given me so many new thoughts, those new neural
 pathways, and amazingly created my brain and heart to do
 new things.*
Thank You that You don't focus on all my faults,
that you're the God who doesn't endlessly nag or scold,
nor will You hold a grudge forever, like some I've known.
*Thank You that You give forgiveness to me—and the power that
 comes only through You to forgive others.*
*As high as the heavens are above the earth, as deep as the ocean,
 as beautiful as the sunrise or sunset, so is Your love.*
I'm learning more about You, Lord, and about Your blessing.
*Now, please, through Your strength, make me the person of
 blessing I want to be.*
*Keep me near to You so that I can be the person of blessing I
 need to be.*
*Help me, even though I might struggle with prayer, to keep
 coming to You.*
I thank You and am grateful beyond words for Your blessing.
I'm ready to be the person of blessing You've called me to become.

Until one is committed there is hesitancy, the chance to draw back, always ineffectiveness. Concerning all acts of initiative (and creation), there is one elementary truth, the ignorance of which kills countless ideas and splendid plans: that the moment one definitely commits oneself, then Providence moves too. All sorts of things occur to help one that would never otherwise have occurred. A whole stream of events issues from the decision, raising in one's favour all manner of unforeseen incidents and meetings and material assistance, which no man could have dreamt would have come his way. I have learned a deep respect for one of Goethe's couplets: "Whatever you can do, or dream you can, begin it. / Boldness has genius, power, and magic in it."

W. H. MURRAY, *The Scottish Himalayan Expedition*

CHAPTER 23

A WHOLE WORLD IS WAITING TO GET IN YOUR BLESSING LINE

You've learned a lot in the previous chapters about missing the Blessing. And we're excited about what all this can mean not just for your healing but also for your potential to go and do something great—great, that is, in the way Jesus defined greatness. Let's look at a picture of Him showing us real greatness, for it is linked with the Blessing as well.

We read in Mark 9 about a time the disciples are arguing about who is the greatest among them. In one of the very best "Gotcha!" moments in Scripture, Jesus asks them, "What were you discussing on the way?"

> But they kept silent, for on the way they had discussed with one another which of them was the greatest. And sitting down, He called the twelve and said to them, "If anyone wants to be first, he shall be last of all and servant of all." And He took a child and placed him among them,

and taking him in His arms, He said to them, "Whoever receives one child like this in My name receives Me; and whoever receives Me does not receive Me, but Him who sent Me."

MARK 9:33-37

We always end our Zoom book clubs by challenging the people who have taken part not just to learn about the Blessing or how to move past missing it but also *to do something great*: to give the Blessing to someone else.

One woman in a recent book club applied this call to blessing children, starting with just one. She was already a second-grade Sunday school teacher at her church, so she had a bit of a captive audience. But she decided to start a tradition at the end of every class.

As the class was ending and the children's parents were coming to pick them up, she had all her students get in what she called her "blessing line." All the kids would line up. Then, one at a time, she would put her hand on the top each child's head or shoulder and speak a word of blessing over the boy or girl.

She'd say something short and sweet, such as "Lord, please bless Caleb this week. You've given him such a wonderful heart" or "Lord, would You bless Stacy this week? She's such a wonderful helper. She always helps people finish their craft and helps me pick up."

And on it would go. All this time, the parents were watching. Her blessing line became just part of what you saw if you were picking up your child. It was a small thing, yet it was powerful and great for each of the kids.

Then one Sunday, after several weeks of seeing her child being blessed each week, a mom jumped into line right behind her daughter. When she got up to the teacher, she asked, "Can you bless me, too? I really need it."

What started with the children in the class ended up including the parents getting blessings as well.

A World of People Who Need *Your* Blessing

There really is a world of people out there who need the Blessing. And God has created you for a purpose—to receive and to give the Blessing in these difficult, challenging days. Many people—if they knew what the Blessing really was, if they saw it being lived out—would want to jump into line to be blessed as well.

Finally: Understand that the people you meet and do life with need *your* blessing. In many cases, if you don't give it to them, they're not going to get it at all.

God has created you for a purpose—to receive and to give the Blessing in these difficult, challenging days.

So keep reading. Keep moving on from missing the Blessing. And keep getting ready to do something great by learning how to give and live the Blessing. In the last chapter, we'll offer you a whole month of suggestions for how you can do just that.

*You have a God who hears you, the power of love behind
you, the Holy Spirit within you, and all of heaven
ahead of you. If you have the Shepherd, you have
grace for every sin, direction for every turn, a candle
for every corner, and an anchor for every storm.*

MAX LUCADO, *Traveling Light:*
Releasing the Burdens You Were Never Intended to Bear

CHAPTER 24

A MONTHLONG JOURNEY FROM MISSING TO RECEIVING, GIVING, AND LIVING THE BLESSING

We take lots of pictures with our phones. Many of us can't remember the last time (if ever) we needed to get the kids dressed up, drive to a studio, and have a family portrait taken. If you can remember that experience, you may know that it was often traumatic. You had to get everyone stuffed into those uncomfortable dress clothes and then labor to create one exact moment when everyone would be sitting still and all smiling at the same time.

But at least there was something positive about that experience. *You were able to go back and look at the proofs.*

You'd wait several weeks.

Go back to the studio.

Then they'd open the folder and lay out what you'd really looked like as a family that day. And many of the pictures weren't ones you wanted to keep.

But the great thing about proofs was they weren't the pictures you had to hang on your wall. In fact, our family had several portrait sittings where we couldn't find a single proof with everyone's eyes open and heads turned the same way. We've even had to retake a portrait to get it right.

Today, many of our phones can autocorrect red eyes or even delete unwanted items in the background. We can use them to make lighting and editing changes to make things look better.

That's what Kari and I want you to do in this last section of the book. We want you to realize that—unless this is the last day of your life—if you missed the Blessing or have failed so far to become the person of blessing you want to be, this doesn't have to be the final picture of your life story.

Perhaps you've struggled to bless and affirm.

You can change that picture.

Perhaps you were missing joy in the pictures of your life story or every one seems filled with looks of anger or hurt.

Those don't have to be the only pictures you're left with—or the ones that define you.

What you know now, from reading this book, is that almighty God sets before us a choice. Life or death. Blessing or curse. And at our very cellular level, we have been fearfully and wonderfully made to create new pictures. To make new connections. To create new neural pathways that change our thinking and hearts. To replace curse with blessing. No matter our age or what's happened in our pasts.

The following devotionals can help you think through, pray through, and apply what you've learned. They're broken into four sections, one week apiece, each with a daily reading. They will walk you back through the high points of what you've read and further encourage you to make the Blessing a daily, purposeful practice.

Week One: On Missing the Blessing (days 1–7)
Week Two: On Receiving the Blessing (days 8–14)

Week Three: On Giving the Blessing (days 15–21)
Week Four: On Living the Blessing (days 22–28)

Feel free to take this book with you to work or on a trip or place it on your pillow in the morning so that at night you remember to pick it up. It may be a blessing to your family to include them in these devotional activities. You might make a commitment with your spouse to read through one short session each night and set aside a time to discuss it the next day.

Most of all, we pray that this daily journey will be another way to help you move past missing the Blessing. We'd love to see you move on, in Christ—with that solid center the Blessing gives you—to receiving, giving, and living the Blessing.

May the Lord bless, keep, and guide you and your loved ones during this month of reading and through every new season of life.

John Trent
Kari Trent Stageberg

Week One: On Missing the Blessing

Day 1

The following is the prayer of a teenage boy. It's a story of missing the Blessing and much more.

DID YOU EVER FAIL, LORD?
No one pays any attention to me
or what I say, Lord.
I'm nobody, I guess.
I haven't done anything important
or made anything
or won anything.
No one listens when I talk,
no one asks my opinion.

I'm just there
like a window
or a chair.

I tried to build a boat once,
but it fell apart.
I tried to make the baseball team,
but I always threw past third base.
I wrote some articles
for our school paper,
but they didn't want them.
I even tried out for the school play,
but the other kids laughed
when I read my lines.
I seem to fail
at everything.

I don't try anymore
because I'm afraid to fail.
And no one likes to fail
all the time.

If only there was something I could do,
something I could shout about,
something I could make
that was my work,
only mine.
And people would say,
"David did that!"
And my parents would say,
"We're proud of you, son!"

But I can't do anything.
Everyone else is so much better
at everything
than I am.
The more I fail
the more it eats away at me
until I feel weak inside.
I feel like I'm nothing.

Lord,
the world seems full of heroes
and idols and important people.

Where are all the failures?
Where are they hiding?
Where are people like me?
Did you ever fail, Lord?
Did you?
Do you know how I feel?
Do you know what it's like
when everyone looks up at you and says:
"He's a failure."
DAVID

For Mature Adults Only[1]

Heartbreaking, isn't it? In many ways, that's where we started this book. Many of us bring with us pictures of having missed the Blessing and more. These are the kinds of pictures this teenager, and many of us, have carried for a long time in our hearts. Take a minute to look at them, won't you?

A boat that fell apart.
Feeling like he can't do anything well.

Baseball tryouts where he made a fool of himself. The coach dismissing him with a shake of his head. The more athletic boys clumped together, whispering, pointing, snickering.

Getting the article back from the editor of the school newspaper. The look of disappointment in David's eyes. The flush of embarrassment over his face.

Tryouts for the school play. David waiting his turn, measuring himself against all who have gone before him, trying to remember his lines, stomach churning as he tucks in his shirt, cinches his belt. It's his turn now, and when he delivers his lines, his voice cracks. On her clipboard, the instructor takes note. So does everyone else.

Do you see what is happening? David is dying, one picture at a time. There is so much subtraction, so little addition. It seems to him that life is far more curse than blessing. He's not alone.

If this boy's life doesn't sound like your own, perhaps it made you think of the kid next door or your own kid. Maybe she's grown now. Or he's an uncle or someone you work with. There's someone like David in all our lives. And he desperately needs a new set of pictures to live by.

David is dying, one picture at a time. There is so much subtraction, so little addition.

Take a moment to think about who that is. If it's you, you know the hurt is real. But know as well that Jesus knew suffering. He knew rejection. He knew subtraction and abandonment by His closest friends as well. Yet *His love and blessing are always there for you.*

For those of us who missed the Blessing, God absolutely knows our hurt and tears. Even more, He is committed to—and gave His Son's life to—reversing the curse. His suffering gives us the choice of new life and a new set of pictures to live by: "For God so loved the world, that He gave His only Son, so that everyone [including *your name here*] who believes in Him will not perish, but have eternal life" (John 3:16).

Lord, thank You that we can be honest about our hurt and pain. Like that sad boy, we've had many chances when we could have been blessed but weren't. When we could have been accepted, valued, chosen, but weren't. That can be hard to live with.

But thank You as well that we don't have to be that hurting child, teenager, or adult who is defined by our losses. Thank You that today we can life up our eyes and see You looking back in love. Right now, in Christ, we can know that we are loved, blessed, held, chosen, adopted, wanted. You do know our pain, Lord Jesus. You suffered a lot of hurt Yourself. Thank You for making life much more than the hurt we've had. Thank You for the new life, blessing, future, and joy You bring.

Day 2

A thirteen-year-old boy and his younger sister had a disagreement over who got to use the home computer one evening, and the boy slapped her. The father grabbed him by the shoulders and demanded, "Why did you do that, son?"

Now, that's usually not a very good question to ask children, particularly younger ones. We will ask something like "Why did you pour out that cereal?" and of course the kid doesn't know why he did it.

But with this boy the question was more meaningful. The father really did wonder why he had done it, and so did the boy. He was not usually physical, especially with his sister. No answer came to him, though, and he only said, "I'm sorry."

About an hour later, the boy came to his dad and said, "I've been thinking about your question, and I think I know the answer."

The father looked at his son, obviously proud of him, and asked him to go on.

"Well," said the boy, "I went to my room to think about it, and I remembered that my math teacher embarrassed me in front of the whole class today. I was so mad at her, but I couldn't do anything about it, so I just kept all those bad feelings inside of me all day. I think I just let them out at Sis."

LINDA AND RICHARD EYRE, *Teaching Your Children Sensitivity*[2]

When we're left with a picture, particularly a painful one like the math teacher left with this boy, it can affect the pictures *we* leave behind. When we're hurt, we get angry. And even though we try our best to keep the anger inside, it can burst out, sometimes at people who in no way deserve it. We need to do more with our anger than just try, in our worldly strength, to hold it back. That's a losing proposition. It's like trying to keep a beach ball underwater. The more determined we are to push it down, the more forceful it is in pushing its way up.

That's why it's so important that we realize that the negative pictures we received really can cause hurt and pain to us and to others. We need to acknowledge the hurt and anger. To exhale. To ask for God's help in being able to forgive. To untie the knots that have bound us for a long time.

We can choose life over death. Blessing over curse.

Take a few minutes to think about the pictures that have made you angry. Maybe that anger has spilled over onto someone else. Did any of these pictures embarrass anyone, humiliate anyone, demean anyone? It doesn't take much. A defiant gesture. A disgusted look. A sarcastic word.

If you've left a picture like that in someone's life, go to the person and talk about it. Ask her what she saw, what he heard, how she felt. Tell him how sorry you are for what you said, what you did, and how you reacted.

Yes, we know that the person who hurt you, in most cases, would *never* do that. He will likely never say he's sorry, apologize, or ask for your forgiveness. But that is his choice.

We can choose life over death. Blessing over curse. We can choose to be the person of blessing God has called us to become.

Lord, You know I've been hurt. You know as well that I've been trying to just push it all deep down inside me. But that's not working and never will. All the hurt, all the anger—I don't want it spilling out anymore onto the lives of people I love. Forgive me for lashing out. And help me, Lord, through Your strength and love, to stop the war inside that I've read about in this book. I'm done with fighting it. Hating back. Hurting others because I've felt so hurt. Your blessing is real, Lord. "If anyone is in Christ, this person is a new creation; the old things passed away; behold, new things have come" (2 Corinthians 5:17). That's real. That's what Your love does and can do in my life. Make me new and a person of love and blessing. I ask for Your love. I ask for Your forgiveness. And Your blessing.

Day 3

The Kilns
6 July 63

Dear Mary

. . . Do you know, only a few weeks ago I realised suddenly that I at last had forgiven the cruel schoolmaster who so darkened my childhood. I'd been trying to do it for years; and like you, each time I thought I'd done it, I found, after a week or so it all had to be attempted over again. But this time I feel sure it is the real thing. And (like learning

*to swim or to ride a bicycle) the moment it does happen it
seems so easy and you wonder why on earth you didn't do it
earlier . . .*

Yours,
Jack

The letter above was written by C. S. Lewis, noted Christian
author and apologist.[3] He wrote it to an American woman he had
met through a letter, and through the course of more than a hundred subsequent letters, they carried on a friendship. The friendship continued for thirteen years, with this letter written just a few
months before he died. In it he recounted the painful childhood
memory of a teacher in an English public school who had bullied
him and all the other boys in his class.

The hurt little boy grew up to be a teacher himself, a well-
respected scholar at a well-respected university. He was a famous
author, writing letters to people across continents to help them as
they struggled with their faith. And he was a strong Christian. Yet
it took him all his life to come to terms with that picture.

That's what we want you to think about today: that someone with such wisdom, faith, and love—a world-class follower of
Jesus—struggled to forgive.

Just as we can.

Take a minute to thumb through the pictures of your past. Does
a picture of someone who has hurt you keep coming to mind? If so,
ask God to shed light on the picture, enabling you to see it through
more compassionate eyes. Then take the picture to the Cross, forgiving as Jesus forgave, and entrusting the injustice, as He did, to
Him who judges righteously (1 Peter 2:23).

*Lord, it isn't easy to forgive. Not after that kind of hurt.
Not with that person. But it doesn't mean I can't become the*

*person of blessing You want me to be. Thank You that great
people of faith and intellect like C. S. Lewis struggled with
certain pictures just like I do at times. But thank You, too,
that we can forgive. And that we—like him—can move
forward and make a difference in people's lives.*

Day 4

The names have been changed, but by and large, what follows is
a true story. It's the story of a father who died too soon to leave
behind many memories. But one was a picture of blessing that
stayed with a young son all his life.

The best thing that happened that day was the second time
Teddy and his father went swimming. . . . Teddy thought
the barrels [that he and his father were swimming toward]
still looked a long way off, and the beach was so far behind
he could hardly recognize his mother and Bean sitting on
it. His arms were beginning to ache, and he was feeling out
of breath. What if he started to drown, he thought? What
if he called for help and his father, who was a little ahead
of him, didn't hear? What if a giant octopus swam up
from below and wrapped him in its slimy green tentacles?
But just as he was thinking these things, his father turned
around and treaded water, waiting for him.

"How about a lift the rest of the way?" Mr. Schroeder
said. So Teddy paddled over and put his arms around his
father's neck from behind, and that was the best part of
the day for him and the part he remembered for many
years afterward. . . .

As he swam out toward the barrels on his father's
back, he . . . knew that there was no place in the whole
Atlantic Ocean where he felt so safe.

PETER BUECHNER, *The Wizard's Tide*[4]

If we missed the Blessing, we missed out on someone turning toward us when we were afraid and needed someone to reach out. Someone to offer to help. Someone to hold on to when we were tired or the fearful pictures came. We need pictures of a father who turns toward us, particularly as we dog-paddle our way through the vast and uncertain ocean that is life. We need someone who makes us feel safe.

Safe in the eyes that look back at us.

Safe in the face that smiles at us.

Safe in the voice that calls to us, "How about a lift the rest of the way?"

That's what Jesus does. As with Peter on the lake (see Matthew 14:22-33), He never lets us sink beneath the waves.

> *Lord, You are our rock and our hiding place. Thank You, Lord, that just as the safest place in all the Atlantic was that father's shoulders, the safest place in all the universe is in Your arms. Carry us forward when we need it. Guard us. Sustain us. We may have missed it in a parent or other loved one. We never will with You. Thank You for being there for us, our Good Shepherd, even in dark, scary times.*

Day 5

There is a popular black-and-white photograph that shows a little boy and girl from the back holding hands as they are walking out of a dark, leafy tunnel and into the shimmering light. If you saw it, I'm sure you'd remember seeing it somewhere.

The father of the children, W. Eugene Smith, took the picture. It's police officer Lucille Burrascano's favorite. Here's why.

He took these children out of a tunnel-effect into the light, two children walking together down the road of life. This is his beautiful wish for joy and lightness and happiness.

It's about the future. They're in motion, and they're hand in hand. When I was working with abused children, this image became even more profound to me, because abused children aren't allowed to be like this. *This* picture became my goal. . . .

For abused children, life is always a tunnel. There's never any light. . . . They are locked into anger and bitterness and fear, and can't go forward. What I love about this picture is that these two children, these two inarticulate adults, these midgets, have taken that step and come *out* of this darkness. . . .

Make this picture a goal, I say. Let your child go forward unscattered, unfettered, unscathed. There's going to be enough chaos in their lives. There's going to be enough tragedy. God knows, it's out there. I tell the mothers, "Now go home and kiss your babies good night. Go out and save some children. They're not going to be babies forever."

LUCILLE BURRASCANO, quoted in *Talking Pictures: People Speak about the Photographs That Speak to Them* by Marvin Heiferman and Carole Kismaric[5]

It's easy to look at the photograph of the boy and girl holding hands as they emerge from the tunnel of leaves and see how it relates to children. But there are tunnels in life through which each of us may someday have to pass. A long tunnel of addiction. A leafy tunnel of changing jobs, changing neighborhoods, changing friends. A dark tunnel of disease, divorce, death.

How do we get through them?

No matter how long the tunnel or how dark or confusing the turns along the way, the surest way to get through is to follow the light. The safest way is to take another person's hand.

Do you have a picture in your mind of somebody who's trapped in a tunnel, somebody who's a little lonely, a little lost, a little scared? Step into the photo, won't you? Take his hand. Walk through it with her. Your companionship through this difficult passage will be a picture the person will never forget.

Lord, I've been in those tunnels. And alone. When a period of trial in my life has seemed to stretch out forever. When the pain has seemed like it's all around me and the light far away. Father, even if I'm there now, let me remember someone today who's in the middle of his or her own tunnel . . . and help that person find Your light and the way out. I know I need Your light and Your blessing. I know You've helped me get out of the tunnels. Now help me heal by reaching out to others as well.

Day 6

Consider this woman recalling the birth of her first child: "I remember taking him to my mom—my mom had not seen him—and I'll never forget the look. It, she, just crushed me. She looked at him as if to say, 'Is that him?'" This woman knew that there was far more to this memory than the moment it captured. Her mother's look was the one she had always received as a child, her mother's attitude, the one that had always met the things she produced. Nothing, in fact, could serve as a better metaphor for the extended nature of this mother-daughter relationship than the memory of that glance.

JOHN KOTRE, *White Gloves: How We Create Ourselves through Memory*[6]

That glance. How many of us have seen it sometime in our lives? From someone important to us. How often has the flashbulb gone off when such a glance was given? And how long has the picture remained in our memories? Can you see it now?

The raising of an eyebrow.

The squinting of the eyes.

The closing of the eyelids.

The flutter of the lashes.

The wrinkling of the forehead.

The pursing of the lips.

The shaking of the head.

The cocking of the neck.

The clucking of the tongue.

The gaping of the mouth.

That glance is captured in a fraction of a second. The picture of that glance endures for a lifetime.

As you read in the earliest chapters of this book, the looks we give others are important. Even more important is the way God looks at us—the way His eyes are there for us. Joy in His face. There are better, healthier, more loving pictures right there in God's gracious eyes if we need them. His love can help us look at others with love as well.

None of us are perfect. But we can begin to practice blessing glances. We can try saying kind things with our eyes and nice things with our faces. We can work on that glimmer in the eye that says, "I'm so proud of you." That smile that says, "You're special." The adoring gaze or special wink we give our loved one that says, "I love you more than words can ever express."

We don't have to be perfect at it. We get tired and frustrated. But if a picture or glance from someone who has hurt you comes back in vivid color, remember that it has no place in your home and shove it back in some bottom drawer.

Lord, I am so glad that, with all the negative looks and pictures that come from missing the Blessing, I have an unshakable, wonderful picture of You. Your eyes and heart and name on me. Your look brings joy, not sorrow or shame, to my heart. I need that look, Lord—that same look You gave while forgiving Peter when he denied You. That look when

*You ascended into heaven that sent Your people away with
great joy. Thank You that Your look says You love me.*

Day 7

Our last day of looking at the hurt that comes from missing the
Blessing brings to mind a picture I (John) just saw. After thirty
years of living in our house, it was time to replace our roof. We
had workmen climbing up, ripping off the old tile, and tossing it
down into a huge dumpster they had placed in our driveway—all
so they could put on the new (expensive) roof we'd (thankfully)
saved for for many years. (*Thank You, Lord, for a wise wife who
saved for a long time.*)

But let's go back to that huge dumpster, because that was the
problem I saw. When the large truck came to pick up a roof's worth
of broken tile and haul it away, the long metal cable struggled to
pull the dumpster up toward the truck bed. It was so heavy that
the truck's front wheels lifted off the ground!

The dumpster was just too heavy for the truck.

There was only one way to remove the dumpster and gain the
freedom to use our driveway and garage again. *We needed a bigger
truck.*

This book and this week may have brought back many painful memories, and we've tried to toss them into the dumpster. But
that's hard to do. To move those kinds of barriers and find that
kind of freedom, we need a bigger helper. We need the greatest
Helper of all to clear away the mess. We need the One who really
can open up a new way of life and never tires of doing so. We read
about this in Isaiah 40:27-31:

Why do you say, Jacob, and you assert, Israel,
   "My way is hidden from the LORD,
      And the justice due me escapes the notice of my God?"
Do you not know? Have you not heard?

The Everlasting God, the LORD, the Creator of the ends
    of the earth
Does not become weary or tired.
His understanding is unsearchable.
He gives strength to the weary,
    And to the one who lacks might He increases power.
Though youths grow weary and tired,
    And vigorous young men stumble badly,
Yet those who wait for the LORD
    Will gain new strength;
    They will mount up with wings like eagles,
    They will run and not get tired,
    They will walk and not become weary.

*Lord, we've looked at many barriers to blessing in this book.
Many of us have missed out on the five elements of the
Blessing. We have come from homes that withheld love and
blessing from us. We have had many negative pictures pile
up, blocking our lives and futures. We're weary and tired of
it all, and we can't move them on our own. We need You,
Jesus. Your love and blessing. For indeed, the only thing
strong enough to break the curse is Your blessing. Help me
remember that You can break down and haul off any barrier.
That You can build something new and honoring and full of
blessing in my life.*

    I'm ready, Lord . . . for my blessing from You.

Week Two: On Receiving the Blessing

Day 8

Our prayer is that, with the Lord's help, these next few days will
become for you one of those attachment moments we've written
about often—a time when God breaks into your life. If you've
said for years, or even just since you picked up this book, "I *never*

got it. I never got the Blessing," we pray that after this week you'll never say that again.

Every day this week, we're going to pray blessings over you. You'll be able to read them, put your name in them in places, and say with full authority, "I *did* get the Blessing. Not growing up. But I did get the Blessing from Kari Stageberg and John Trent. *And* from the Lord."

If you were here with us, we'd have you sit in a comfortable chair with a low back. Kari would stand on one side, asking for permission and then putting her hand on your shoulder. And I (John) would be standing next to her with my hand on her shoulder. Then both of us would take turns reading these blessings over you each day.

As you read these blessings (which we'd encourage you to do out loud), hear our voices joining yours. And know that there's someone else in the room too.

Remember how we talked about Jesus' being seated in the heavenly places and how He invites us—amazingly, supernaturally—to sit right next to Him *right now*? His is the other voice joining in as you read these blessings.

We pray you'll hear in these words the voice of the One who has always loved you. Who will always be there for you. Who has lifted you out of all the hurt and pain and will never leave you or forsake you.

Here, then, are the first words of blessing for you:

Lord Jesus, thank You that You're here. Wherever we are right now, we are also right next to You in the heavenly places.

With this promise in mind, we don't enter into this week of blessings lightly. This is a time to know that there is something more than just words being spoken here. We're asking You, Jesus, to bless _____.

Lord, we have said of the Blessing, "I've missed it. I never got the Blessing." But on this _____ day of _____, help _____ know that whatever has been blocking him or her from receiving the Blessing in the past doesn't have to define him or her anymore. That whatever curse or barrier was set up by a parent or other person in his or her past can be broken down right now.

We know that the word curse *in Scripture means "to dam up the stream," to be left with just a muddy trickle when we need a lot more. But You, Jesus, sat down with a broken and thirsty woman at the well. Five times she'd had someone important walk away from her. Cut her off. Toss her aside. Lord, we've had people walk away from us, too. So much subtraction and loss of hope and life.*

But we believe You can break through all the hurt. You can lift away any barrier. You can give _____ a new, clear path to travel. Right now, Lord, as You did for the woman at the well, You offer living water for our journeys.

And on this first day of _____'s blessing, may he or she know that this blessing is being spoken over him or her. May he or she know that these words convey Your blessing.

May this be the last day of _____'s inner struggle to know he or she is valuable. May he or she really know that Kari and I are with him or her in spirit and faith, praying this for him or her. May he or she truly know that You, Jesus, can break down any barrier, and that You've given him or her strengths and gifts to use to make a difference in this world. And right now, will You bring hope and healing and love, no matter what's happened in the past. For that we're grateful, and we choose to believe that this day and this week the curse ends and Your blessing begins.

Day 9

Pray this for yourself:

Lord, it's day two of having words of blessing poured over me. Once again, I put my name here as I listen to Your blessing:
_____.

 Lord Jesus, You have always poured out Your blessing on those You love, a blessing such as You gave Your spiritual family on Your last day on earth. You blessed them even as You were being lifted up into heaven. Your words brought them great joy that day. And words of blessing can bring joy to my heart as well.

 You know my story surrounding touch, Lord. But I also know that Your touch brings healing. Your touch brings hope. That's the reason the hemorrhaging woman sought You out—why many sought just to reach out and touch You and finally become whole.

 The apostle John wrote of "what was from the beginning, what we have heard, what we have seen with our eyes, what we have looked at and touched with our hands" (1 John 1:1). Lord, if I had been there with You when You were on earth, and if I had reached out to You, You would have reached back, given Your touch, taken my hand. Welcomed me. Changed me.

 Lord, I may have missed this element of the Blessing, but You didn't withhold it from the children who were pushed away by Your disciples. Nor did You keep it from the one child You held in Your arms and blessed.

 And now, Lord, may I know in my heart of hearts that You really are able to hold me tight. That's the picture used in Psalms about Your great love and blessing. May these words, from Your Word, in the wonderfully readable Message *paraphrase, bring healing and the reality of Your tender, loving touch:*

I can see now, GOD, that your decisions are right. . . .
Oh, love me—and right now!—hold me tight!
    just the way you promised.
Now comfort me so I can live, really live;
    your revelation is the tune I dance to.
PSALM 119:75-77, MSG

Day 10

Here's another blessing to pray for yourself:

Lord, it's wonderful that You speak words of blessing over me. I've had such words withheld and angry, mocking, belittling, and shameful words shouted at me.

I've heard all kinds of hurtful, even hateful, words. I know it's true, as it says in Your Word, that the tongue can be a fire, carrying with it a world of unrighteousness (James 3:6). That's frightening, Lord. I don't want to be burned again by hurtful words.

But what casts out the fear of negative words, and anything else, is Your perfect love, which casts out fear. As I put my name here—_____—help me hear from You words of affirmation, courage, hope, and comfort. May I know the truth of Psalm 119:50 today: "This is my comfort in my misery, that Your word has revived me." Thank You for blessing me today with uplifting, loving words.

Day 11

Pray this today:

Lord, I don't think I've ever heard so many blessings prayed for me. But on this fourth day of blessing, with Jesus sitting beside me and Kari and John alongside me in spirit, may I begin to see the strengths You've put in my life.

*Lord, You have placed me right where You want me
(1 Corinthians 12:18). You've given me gifts and strengths to
help others. Help me, Lord, see and live out those strengths.
Then help me grab hold of more of Your purpose for my life.*

*Lord, help me know today the high value Jesus places
on me. Not because I've earned it, deserve it, or demand it.
I know it's Your free gift, through grace and by faith, that
has saved me. And it's You, Lord, who can unleash the gifts
and strengths You've given me to serve and bless others. I was
created to be part of Your body! I'm a part of Your family!
People need me, and I can help and bless them. Thank You,
Jesus, for making me useful, needed, and able to make a
difference in others' lives. That's a huge blessing from You.*

Day 12

It's day five of blessings being spoken over you. There's hardly a
day that goes by without someone on my phone or on television
shouting that the world is ending for some reason. War. Pollution.
Climate change. So, for your blessing and reassurance, pray the
following:

*On this fifth day of blessing, I again put my name here:
_____. Lord, may You help me know that You're not
done with me or our world. There really is a future and a
hope that You promise. You alone, Lord, know the future,
and it's a future where I am wanted.*

*Your Word tells me, too, that You're coming back to set up
a new heaven and earth—a place more special than any we
can find today. A place where there are no tears, no sorrow,
no sickness. A place with You, Lord.*

*You say a lot, Lord, about the inheritance You've given
me and all who are Your children. About the dwelling places
You've set up for us. It may be decades before we reach our
heavenly home. But until then, may I know that while there*

may be sorrow in the evening, joy—Your fullness of joy—comes in the morning (Psalm 30:5). And because of Your blessing, I can bless others in powerful ways. So may my eyes be lifted up today to see You, Lord, and the special future only You can bring.

Day 13

Today, pray this part of the Blessing for yourself:

Jesus, thank You for how committed You are to being there for me forever. No one else can say that and have it be totally true. Even my best friends and the person who loves me most will one day move from earth to heaven, or out of my reach and touch.

But You, Lord, will always be there, letting me sit beside You. Your name, Your eyes, and Your heart are there for me forever. That kind of "only God" commitment is beyond huge and helpful and powerful.

May I find in all these blessings the comfort and reality of Your Word: "For He Himself has said, 'I WILL NEVER DESERT YOU, NOR WILL I EVER ABANDON YOU'" (Hebrews 13:5). And I don't even have to read those words a hundred times to believe them!

Day 14

Whenever Kari and I (John) sit down to write, we always pick a place where there's an empty chair in front of or beside us. And whenever we look up, we picture someone sitting in that chair. Today it's *you* sitting in that chair.

We wish we really could look you in your eyes and say with our eyes and hearts how glad we are you've picked up this book. If any of it has helped you get past missing the Blessing, you would see the joy on our faces.

Then we'd walk over and, with your permission, put a hand on your shoulder and pray one more prayer of blessing over you:

> *Well, Lord, it's been a week of _____'s being blessed. We pray that one day, even though it may not be until we're all in heaven, we'll really get to meet face-to-face. We'll celebrate together the truth that Your Spirit and Your love have been in these words of blessing, because they reflect Your heart and Your Word.*
>
> *And on the day when we do meet, we can't wait to hear how Your blessing has made such a difference in the rest of _____'s life.*
>
> *It's You, Lord, who has been here all the time. And while we're stopping now, You never stop blessing those You love. Thank You for that, and for blessing _____, and may each new day, and every new season of life, be different because of Your blessing.*

That's your blessing! You've now had a week's worth of our best effort, through prayer and asking God for the right words, to help you be able to say, "*I got it! I did get the Blessing!*" Yes, you may have missed it growing up. But now you can say, *I have Your blessing, Lord, and the blessing of two friends named Kari and John, whom I'll get to meet one day, whether it's running through an airport, at a conference, or for sure in heaven. So now I really am free and ready to go out and change the world—starting with one person who needs my blessing.*

Week Three: On Giving the Blessing

Day 15

You've spent one week reviewing some thoughts, Scriptures, prayers, and insights to help with the very real pain of missing the Blessing. And now you've spent a second week receiving the Blessing.

Jesus also got the Blessing (for example, see Matthew 3:13-17), but He didn't just receive it. He also *gave* blessings to many others. Likewise, this week we're going to ask you to move your focus from what you missed to how to give your blessing to someone who needs it from you.

And today, your assignment is the starting point.

We're asking you to prayerfully pick a person you're going to meet (even if it's over a video call) and bless. An obvious choice may be your child. (If you have more than one, start with one, but commit to blessing all of them.)

Perhaps you'll choose to bless your spouse or the person you're dating or that roommate who never got the Blessing or even your own parents.

During the height of COVID, we received a letter and a picture from a young woman who had longed for her father's blessing all her life. Now there was a worldwide pandemic, and increasingly, those most at risk were those in nursing homes, like her father.

Pandemic or not, she would give him her blessing even though he had never given it to her.

She didn't want to lose him without saying or doing something. And that's why, in reading *The Blessing*, she decided she needed to bless him.

Pandemic or not, she would give him her blessing even though he had never given it to her.

He was locked away in a nursing home, but she bravely talked the staff into making an exception (of sorts) for her and her father. The picture she sent was of her and her dad sitting on folding chairs in a grass field behind his home. Her husband took the photo right in the middle of her blessing her father. She was leaning forward, reading from a piece of paper. Her father was about ten feet away. Completing the scene were some nurses standing near him.

She had done what we're asking you to do this week. She had

picked someone to bless. In her case, it was a father whom she didn't want to lose without his knowing she loved him—and that he had her blessing! Then she literally followed the script you'll see in each day that follows this week. She chose a strength that she saw and felt God had given him. Then she came up with a word-picture object that helped clarify that strength. (As you'll see, that's just a keepsake object or memorial marker to remember this time.) Finally, she closed her blessing with words of genuine commitment and a prayer.

To go back to her picture, she wrote that everything had been set up on her blessing day. And though she read her father her letter of blessing, you can just speak your blessing or video record it on your phone.

Her father was so moved that he got up, ignored the protesting nurses, and ran over to her and hugged her! For the first time, he even told her he loved her! (No one got COVID by hugging either.)

Of course, we can't promise your blessing experience will go as well as this. But like this woman, just trust God and start by praying about and choosing—*today*—who it is you're going to bless. (Note that you can bless a positive influence, too, not just someone who has hurt you.)

On this day, _____, I am choosing to bless _____.

Day 16

You've read how God's eyes are on us, how He looks for things in our lives that He can strongly support. And part of what He does in blessing us is give us strengths and gifts, even spiritual gifts (for example, see 1 Corinthians 12:1-31). These gifts and strengths aren't just for our own benefit but are things that can build up the church and others!

So today we want you to think about a strength or gift or

character trait that you've seen in the person you've chosen to bless. With my (John's) father, it had to do with his courage and service to our country. For you, it may be a person's sensitivity or caring heart, gift of leadership, or willingness to serve or sacrifice for others.

Just don't pick a physical trait like *Well, she has big hair!* Take time right now to come up with a strength, character trait, or spiritual gift you believe God has given the person.

The strength or gift God has given the person I'm blessing is

_____.

Day 17

You've chosen a person, and you've identified a strength or gift you can build into your blessing. Eventually, you'll use that to speak your blessing. But on this day, we encourage you to think about an object or a picture or even a story that illustrates the character trait you picked.

For example, let's say the strength you see in the person you want to bless is *compassion*. In fact, you've seen this trait lived out in her life since she was three years old. Even as a child, she would try to help and encourage other kids. As she grew up, she would look for ways to comfort anyone around her who was hurting!

So if compassion is the strength you would pick (and there may be others, but pick just one), now think of something small, like an object or picture, that illustrates the strength.

Let's stay with this person who has always been compassionate. In fact, let's say she's grown up and is a nurse today. (What a shock someone like this would want a profession where she could help ease pain!)

You think about something that pictures compassion, and what you come up with is the stethoscope she's always wearing around her neck. Every time she goes to work, she's wearing it. So when you bless her, you're going to bring with you a picture of a stethoscope. (You don't have to go buy a new one; a picture is fine.)

As you build out your blessing, it could sound something like this:

> *Maria, I want you to know that for years I've seen you be a wonderful example of compassion to others. When anyone was hurting around you, you'd be there for them. And while you don't wear this when you're outside the hospital [show her your picture of the stethoscope], you're always listening to what's going on in someone's heart. You always care about the person. It's like you're God's stethoscope to help others.*

This is just an example. And we know this may be something that takes most of the week to come up with. So yes, if you get totally stuck, you can call in a creative friend to help you come up with a picture or object of the strength you've picked.

But don't skip this.

Almost every time a blessing was given in Scripture, the person giving the Blessing linked his words of blessing with a picture. For example, go to Genesis 27:27: "See, the smell of my son is like the smell of a field which the LORD has blessed." This is a picture of the smell of the harvest, which is a great smell to someone who works the ground and a great way of linking a picture with the affirmation and praise of a son. Whenever Jacob smelled that harvest smell, he'd think, *That's the way my father looks at me, like I'm a prize-winning harvest!*

And every time Maria puts on her stethoscope, she'll think, *I'm God's stethoscope!*

Gary Smalley and I (John) wrote a book called *The Language of Love* that expands on creating word-pictures, but you don't have to go as deep as we do there to give a blessing. Just think of an object or a picture that reflects the person's strength and can help you explain it.

Day 18

You've picked the person, come up with a strength, and after hard work (we're proud of you!), found a picture to help signify your praise. Now add to your spoken blessing your genuine commitment to *be there* to bless him or her.

Say things like "I want you to know that you have my blessing—today and tomorrow and every day the Lord gives me life and breath."

We've talked a lot about attachment in this book. *Attachment* is a synonym for *blessing* in many ways. The moment the enduring, forever commitment of God breaks into your heart, it brings a change of epic proportions. It secures the bond and blessing God gives you. And when someone hears that you're committed to him or her forever, your blessing can have much the same effect!

So, this day, work on writing out a rough draft of your blessing. From the beginning, it could sound something like this:

Hannah, today I want to speak some words over you and give you my blessing. I want you to know that you have my blessing. That you are loved. That I love you. That you are enough. That you are incredibly important to me.

And I want you to know that I think God has given you many awesome strengths, one of which is that you're very determined. You never give up on things or people or school or the Lord. You never give up, just as Jesus never gives up on us.

Here's a picture of what I mean. It's a really cute French bulldog that's being tossed around because he won't let go of a rope. That's you, Hannah. You're such a great friend, relative, wife, mother, and worker. You hang on to others when many people would just walk away.

And now, finally, I want you to know that as long as the Lord gives me strength and breath, I will bless you and always love you.

This is just an example. You can write any blessing you want. Now you've picked someone, you've come up with a strength and an image to reinforce it, and you've added in that you're not going anywhere. There are only two more things to do.

Day 19

On this day, what we're asking you to do will be short, but you can take as long as you want or need to do it. Please pray about your blessing in two ways. First, pray it will be received in a way that honors the person and the Lord. And second, pray that your expectations will be set on having done something important, not on how the person responds.

Unmet expectations are like sulfuric acid. If your expectation is that the person will jump up and down, cry, thank you, or whatever you picture, realize that this may not happen. And that needs to be okay. You're doing this because an incredibly powerful way to move past missing the Blessing is to bless others. It's your calling! Your job!

Unmet expectations are like sulfuric acid.

So pray that you're doing this because you're called to bless and because the person needs your blessing. But understand that the person may not acknowledge it or react with tears or profuse thank-yous or *anything*. But again, you're not doing it to get something but to give a gift.

She may sit still.

He may run past the nurses into your arms as the father did during COVID.

She may tear up.

He may look away.

There's no telling what will happen. But let me (John) end with one story that's more about what happened to the one blessing than to the one being blessed.

Cindy and I led a couples' class for a number of years in our church. And each year, we'd get the people in the class to do what we're asking you to do—pick someone and give a blessing. In this case, since it was a family class, we asked them to bless their children.

One year, a firefighter dad went along with it reluctantly.

On the day the parents were to bless their children, the class would meet in the church gym right after the last Sunday service. We'd start with a potluck and then let the kids run around until they were worn out. Next, I'd call everyone together and announce that the families were to spread out around the gym. It was time for something special for each child there. Finally, after this special time, we'd all have ice cream to celebrate.

Off went the families, flopping down all over and around the gym. I'd walk around taking pictures of the parents blessing their kids.

On this particular day, after all the activities and ice cream, a big, strapping firefighter came up to me in tears. He gave me a rescue-someone-from-a-burning-building bear hug and told me what his son had just told him.

"John, I knew my two boys knew that I loved them. I've told them a bunch of times. So, frankly, I thought this was kind of a waste of time. But I read my older son his blessing that his mom and I wrote, *and he started crying!*"

He continued: "I couldn't figure out what was going on. And then my son said to me, 'Do you really feel that way about me, Dad?' How could he have missed it? How could he have not known?!"

And he cried some more.

"I'm so glad we did this."

There are times, when a blessing is given, that a child or other loved one will hear your message in a different, often more important way than ever before. So your blessing may indeed help fill a hole or close a loop for someone who really needs such a blessing.

But again, your expectations should be on giving it and what that means for you, not on receiving something back. And even if the person doesn't respond right then, perhaps a week or even a year or more later, he or she might pull you aside and tell you how important your blessing was.

Whatever happens, you're doing your job and giving your blessing.

God's Word does not return void. If you've prayed and sought to bless the person, then whatever happens, God will honor it.

Day 20

Today you need to pick the time you're going to bless the person you've chosen and then go do it. Maybe you go early to a ball game, when almost no one is in the stands, and give him your blessing. Maybe there's a nearby park your daughter loves to play at, and after she's gotten out all the wiggles, you give her a juice box and your blessing.

It doesn't have to be fancy or expensive or done on a cruise. Just pick a semi-quiet place, at a good time for everyone, and trust the Lord for whatever happens.

Lord, I've chosen _____ *as the time to give my blessing.*

The moment has come—go give your blessing.

Day 21

On this day, we want you to record what happened when you gave your blessing. What it meant to you. What it meant to the other person. Big or little. Helpful for him or more helpful for you. Whatever happened, you prayed for whom to bless, and you spent time building out a blessing. That may have been more than your parents ever did for you. But you did it. You had the courage to speak it over her.

That's one down, and when the word gets out that you're really good at this blessing thing, get ready for a world in need of your blessing.

We've finished week three. We have just one more week to offer some final thoughts about maintaining and living the Blessing in the days to come.

Week Four: On Living the Blessing

Day 22

What does a life of blessing look like if you've never seen it up close and personal? Just look around now that you're becoming aware of the five elements of the Blessing and how important pictures of blessing really are.

You'll see that they come from imperfect people, insensitive people, impatient people.

People like you and like me.

People like Marjorie Holmes. Many of her books are books of prayers that ask forgiveness for her mistakes and for the grace to keep from making the same mistakes again. Because she kept on her knees, she kept giving pictures of blessing to those she loved.

That's where pictures of blessing can often be found—on our knees. Take a minute to pray through one of Marjorie's prayers, pausing here and there to personalize it, thinking about specific things in your relationships with your own children.

Please teach me to talk to my children. With patience, good humor, sympathy and understanding (insofar as it is *possible* for an adult to understand his children).

And teach me to listen to them in a way that will make them want to talk to me.

I am often baffled by the things they say, shocked by the expressions they use. It sometimes upsets me to know they have the ideas they express.

Then I realize that this is the only way we can hope to bridge the differences between our generations. This frank, free exchange of thoughts.

Help me to keep my emotions out of it, Lord.

Don't let me get my feelings hurt; don't let me get mad. Keep me from sentimental comparisons (how much harder we had things at their age, how respectful and considerate we were of our parents). Guard me against faultfinding and accusations of ungratefulness.

Oh, God, teach me to talk to my children with tact and common sense.

Let me be open to their arguments; don't let me pretend to know all the answers. Let me be honest with them. Don't let me compromise my values. But don't let me be arrogant either. Don't let a desire to be right dominate my desire for genuine communication.

Let love, genuine love, pervade our conversations. Let laughter give it joy and flavor.

Lord, teach me to talk, and to listen, to my children so that they will always want to come back.

MARJORIE HOLMES, "Teach Me to Talk to Them"[7]

Day 23

Being a person of blessing doesn't mean being pious or super-spiritual or perfectionistic. It can mean looking for meaningful ways to have fun with those you love, creating blessing moments in outside-the-box ways!

There's a wonderful, true story of a man who left behind an unforgettable picture for his wife and kids, who were leaving for a family vacation. They were leaving without him because he had to stay behind and work, but he helped them plan in meticulous detail every day of the camping trip. The trip was to start at their home in Montgomery, Alabama. They were to drive to California, travel up and down the West Coast, and then make their way back to Montgomery.

Knowing their entire route, their camping sites, and their times of arrival, he pinpointed the precise time they would be crossing the Great Divide. Then he arranged to fly to the nearest airport and took a cab to take him to the place on the highway where every car had to pass. Once there, he sat by the roadside for several hours, waiting for their station wagon to come into sight. When it did, he stepped onto the road and put his thumb out to hitchhike a ride.

The family, as you could well imagine, got the surprise of their lives when they saw him there, waiting for them. Imagine the laughter. Imagine the conversations. Imagine the memories.

A friend asked him why he went to all that trouble. "Well," he replied, "someday I'm going to be dead and when that happens I want my kids and my wife to say, 'You know, Dad was a lot of fun.'"[8]

But you're thinking, *I'm just not funny or spontaneous.* That's fine. Like this man, try planned spontaneity. Often our lives are so busy that we don't have time even to think about leaving or giving a blessing. So what's wrong with *scheduling* a time of affirmation? Plan a surprise party for your spouse—not a birthday or anniversary party, just an "I love you, and look at all these other people who do too" party. Or a "spontaneous" breakfast with each child . . . planned and noted on your calendar two weeks before. Make it a time to tell your kids that you love them and that today and every day they have your blessing.

Schedule a time of closeness this week.

None of us have forever.

How could you pray, plan, and schedule to bless someone today?

Day 24

Listen, son, I am saying this as you lie asleep, one little paw crumpled under your cheek and the blonde curls stickly wet on your forehead. Just a few moments ago, I sat, reading my paper in the library, and a stifling wave of remorse swept over me. Guiltily I came to your bedside.

These are the things I was thinking, son: I had been cross to you. I scolded you as you were crossing the street because you didn't look both ways before coming over to see me; I didn't like it, and told you so when you just gave your face a dab with the towel. I took you to task for not cleaning your shoes. I called angrily when you threw some of your things on the floor.

At breakfast I found fault too. You spilled things. You gulped down your food. You put your elbows on the table. You spread butter too thick on your bread. And as you started off to play, and I made for my bus, you turned and waved a hand and called, "Goodbye, Daddy," and I frowned and said in reply, "Hold your shoulders back."

Then it began all over again in the late afternoon. As I came up the road I spied you, down on your knees, playing marbles. There were holes in your stockings. I humiliated you before your boy friends by marching you straight to the house ahead of me. Stockings were expensive—and if you had to buy them, you'd be more careful . . .

Do you remember later, when I was reading in the library, how you came in timidly, with a sort of hurt look in your eyes? When I glanced up over my paper, impatient at the interruption, you hesitated at the door, and I snapped, "What do you want?"

You said nothing, just ran across in one tempestuous plunge, threw your arms around my neck and kissed me. And then you were gone, pattering up the stairs.

Well, son, it was shortly afterward that my paper slipped from my hands and a terrible, sickening feeling came over me. What has habit been doing to me? The habit of finding fault, or reprimanding? . . . It was not that

I didn't love you; it was that I expected too much of you. I was measuring you by the yardstick of my own years.

There's so much that is good and fine in your little character. It didn't matter what I said, you came in with a spontaneous burst of childish emotion, and rushed across the room to kiss me goodnight. Nothing else matters tonight, son. I have come to your bedside in the darkness, and I have knelt there, ashamed! . . .

Tomorrow, son, I'll be a real daddy. I'll be kind and thoughtful. I'll laugh when you laugh, and cry when you cry. Don't worry about me, son. I'll remember how important you are, and I'll remember who you are.

I'm afraid I've visualized you as a man. Yet, as I look at you now, son, peacefully sleeping in your little bed, I see that you are still a baby. Yesterday you were in your mother's arms, your head on her shoulder. I have asked too much.

I have expected you to be a man, son, and you're only a little boy.

My little boy.

W. LIVINGSTON LARNED, "Father Forgets"[9]

As the days pass and you look at your little boy or girl—at your older brother or younger sister, at your arthritic mother or aging father, at your pastor or youth worker or school administrator—don't be afraid to apologize. The Blessing was never about being perfect. Don't just rehearse it in your mind or confess it in your prayers by the bedside of the one you've hurt. Pick the right time to talk about it, but do talk about it.

No matter what anybody tells you, apologizing isn't a sign of weakness.

No matter what anybody tells you, apologizing isn't a sign of weakness.

It's a sign of strength.

And it leaves behind a *great* picture of blessing!

Day 25

My wife and I once asked a group of older people to think of one autobiographical object from their past. They were to write it down in big letters on a sheet of paper, pin the paper on their chest, and walk around the room. Pretty soon they were sporting signs saying "buttonhook," "old-fashioned pen," "match," "fishing pole," "Hershey bar," "tricycle," and much more. . . .

One of the women had written "coral elephant" on her piece of paper. She had come from a poor family that couldn't afford new clothes or jewelry for its children. Around the sixth grade, the girl became fascinated with a teacher, a young, attractive woman who always wore beautiful things. One day it was a piece of jewelry, a coral elephant pin, and throughout that day the girl couldn't take her eyes off it. After school she lingered to get a better look and tell the teacher how pretty it was. At the end of the school year, the teacher gave the girl that pin. "It was my most prized possession," the woman said with tears in her eyes. And yet, several years ago, she lost it in a move. All she has left is its memory, and a story that could symbolize her life.

JOHN KOTRE, *White Gloves: How We Create Ourselves through Memory*[10]

Remember my shadow box and asking you to come up with your own in an earlier chapter? One of the most powerful things about an object is that it symbolizes something. Here, a pin symbolized a teacher's fondness for her student and her student's love for her. It was prized when the girl first received it. As she grew older, it was prized even more—so much so that years later the mere memory of it brought tears.

When the person the object symbolizes is gone, the symbol keeps talking. It keeps reminding us of the relationship, of how it has shaped us and is shaping us still.

How is the language of your heart being translated? What objects in your relationships with others symbolize what the people mean to you?

A bowl of ice cream? A box of chocolates?

A game of racquetball? A Saturday of garage sales?

A board game? A music box?

When you're gone, what symbols will be left behind to remind others of you?

Day 26

These little photographs were taken many years ago on my father's wonderful high wood terrace. . . . He is sitting with my uncle, Carl Sandburg, and they are talking, while in the background, my daughter, Francesca, dances. These men have been devoted friends since Carl married my father's sister Lilian. The photographs don't have great artistic merit, but they hold an awful lot for me. As those two brilliant men carried on their discussion, every once in a while, they would comment about what my daughter was doing. . . .

I treasure these photographs because these two men, who are deep in talk, are aware of my daughter. To both of them, children were important and were to be dealt with at any time. They always gave the children the satisfaction of knowing that, and in turn, they received pleasure from watching them.

To me, the reality of these photographs talks about why we are here—to care for each other, to value each other—that's the feeling these small photos evoke for me.

MARY STEICHEN CALDERONE, quoted in *Talking Pictures: People Speak about the Photographs That Speak to Them* by Marvin Heiferman and Carole Kismaric[11]

It was amazing to this mother that two grown-up, important men would take note and look at her daughter with high value. What's amazing to us is how many times it's something small like this that gets noticed—something that can have a profound impact on a person's life. Often, as you seek to live and give the Blessing, it will be the small things where you value and bless someone that can and will change lives.

Consider the picture I saw at Young Life's Frontier Ranch one summer.

Young Life hosts incredible youth camps. This one was held on the side of Mount Princeton, a fourteen-thousand-foot peak in the Collegiate Peaks in Colorado. They wear out the high schoolers with raft and climbing trips, horse rides, and amazing outdoor cookouts.

When I brought my Young Life club from Dallas, Texas, to Frontier Ranch, most meals were in a huge dining room. The Young Life work crew, all college students, would bring in food, sing, and do skits during dinner. But something happened at the table next to me. It was something quiet, a small way to bless someone. And it changed a high schooler's life that week.

The speaker was the president of Young Life at the time, Bob Mitchell. He had done a great job of talking about Jesus. But his messages weren't what changed the young man's life.

It was what Bob Mitchell did in talking to the camp cook.

The meals that week were outstanding. And a key reason was Goldbrick. Goldbrick (whose actual name was Andrew Delaney) was a huge African American. In the Army in World War II, he had cooked his way through France, all the way to the fall of Germany.

Goldbrick had started out cooking for one camp. But as the years went by, he became the head cook for all Young Life camps. His wife joined him in the kitchen as well.

He'd walk around to check on the tables, and every kid there knew and loved Goldbrick.

This was 1972, and he was our cook at Frontier. Every evening, he would walk over to Bob Mitchell's table—again, the man who was both the speaker and the president of the whole ministry. In short, his boss. Goldbrick would check on the menu for the next day and ask if any changes were needed.

Often, as you seek to live and give the Blessing, it will be the small things where you value and bless someone that can and will change lives.

But every time he got to the table, Bob Mitchell would stand up and have Goldbrick sit down in his chair. It was probably the only time since preparing breakfast early that morning that he'd gotten off his feet. And Bob would stand and listen to him, answer questions, and pour him something to drink while he sat.

That was it.

Bob was just blessing someone with a few minutes to rest before a short night. Then Goldbrick would be back to feeding hundreds of hungry high schoolers the next day. It wasn't something small, however, to the young man I'd brought from Dallas.

The last night of camp, they had what they called a "Say So." After the last talk by Bob Mitchell, an invitation for kids to come to Christ was always given. Then Bob would open things up for anyone who wanted to to say something about his or her week at camp.

A number of kids stood up and said they'd trusted in Jesus that week. Others thanked their counselor or Bob. Or they said something they thought was great about camp. But then the young man from Dallas stood up.

He was quiet for a long time. Then he said, "Well, I don't mean to be offensive, but I didn't really get into all the talks. But then I saw something. Our table was right next to Mr. Mitchell's. Every night, I saw Goldbrick come over."

And then he talked about what he'd seen Bob Mitchell doing. He was talking now to Bob, and he said, "I'm not a hundred percent sure what it means to be a Christian yet. But I gave my life to Jesus tonight. Because if that's what a Christian does, I want to be one."

We hope you'll keep that story in mind as you give and live the Blessing. It's probably not that huge thing you do to bless that will change lives. It's living as if others really matter. Valuing them. Blessing them. Pulling a chair out for them. And someone sees . . .

That's the power of a picture.

That's the power of the Blessing.

It makes us feel something.

That's the power in the pictures we leave behind, the power to bless or to curse.

Day 27

There's a delightful children's book that expresses tender and poignant thoughts on what we've been talking about for the past month. The book is titled *The Memory Box*.[12] It's the story of a boy's relationship with his grandfather. When the grandfather learns he has Alzheimer's disease, he wants to make sure the important memories won't be forgotten. That's the catalyst for the creation of the Memory Box.

"It was your Great-Gram who told me about the Memory Box," Gramps said, staring at the sunset sky. "It's a special box that stores family tales and traditions. An old person and a young person fill the box together. Then they store it in a place of honor. No matter what happens to the old person, the memories are saved forever."

For the rest of the grandson's vacation, the two of them remember everything they can. The times they fish together, pick blueberries together. The time they watch as a raccoon eats a trayful of cookies Gram has set on the picnic table to cool.

It was Grampa's job to add photos and souvenirs to the Memory Box. He found a picture of my second birthday party when I had taken a bite off the top of the cake. There was a shot of Gram in her wedding dress with flowers in her hair, and one of Dad in his football uniform when he still *had* hair. Another was of Gramps and Mom the day he had taught her to ride a bike. She had ridden it, too. Right over his foot!

As the summer progresses, so does the Alzheimer's. The grandfather begins to forget things, gets lost in the woods, talks to people who aren't there. One minute he seems fine; another minute he might be reliving a day of his childhood. As he deteriorates, the Memory Box becomes more important to both of them.

When Gramps woke up, he called me. I stood at his bedroom door. He sat on the bed.

"Did Gram tell you about this useless old man? And how he needs to find a home for special things like this?" He handed me the old fishing knife from the shed. "I forgot the sheath, so I went back . . . and got lost."

"Thanks," I whispered, holding the knife the way Gramps had taught me. My own, very first knife. I'd always wanted one. *This* one. But now it didn't seem so important.

"Your Mom's going to hurt," Gramps said. "When it gets bad, bring out the Memory Box. Show her what I remember."

Summer vacation ends, and it's time for the boy to return home. He hugs his grandparents goodbye. He hugs his grandpa especially hard. And when his grandma hugs him, she turns her head to his ear.

"Add things to the Memory Box you want Gramps to remember," she whispered as she handed it to me. "And bring it with you next summer. We'll need it, you and I."

The boy's parents come to take him home. When they drive off, the boy waves to his grandparents, thinking about his summer there and already looking forward to the next. The book ends with a final thought from the boy.

As the car hit the top of the hill, I watched Gramps slowly disappear into the horizon. And I hugged my Memory Box.

Day 28

Here it is, our last day of devotionals—our last time to suggest something we hope will give you a final dose of encouragement to keep moving from missing to receiving, giving, and living the Blessing. And this suggestion is something you can encourage others to take part in as well.

We'd love for you to take part in something that, Lord willing, launched for the first time on November 24, 2024. That was the Sunday before Thanksgiving. We hope that by the time you read this it will have become an official holiday—much more significant than National Fish Taco Day on January 25 or National Squirrel Appreciation Day on January 21.

We'd like you to take part in National Blessing Day. It will always be on the Sunday before Thanksgiving, and our goal is to see it spread from churches to communities to homes and children of all ages, all across our great country. (And yes, we've already been contacted to launch an International Blessing Day as well!)

Our prayer for you is that in reading this book you've realized how deep Jesus' love and blessing is in your life. How powerful God's love is to reverse the curse. And how His love can free you to move past missing the Blessing to receiving, giving, and living it out each day.

May each day in your home be an occasion for a Blessing Day. And may God's love continue to hold you tight and wrap you in the Blessing that Jesus offers to you and all of us.

Acknowledgments

Special acknowledgments need to go to two couples who have done a lot to help launch, unleash, and empower us to take the message of the Blessing worldwide. We are so grateful to Jim and Pam McGuire and Josh and Amy Sherrard for their prayers, friendship, and unshakable love during what have been two of the most challenging years of our lives.

And to our friend of friends Larry Weeden. Larry is a world-class editor who worked on the very first edition of *The Blessing* and on this book as well. Thank you, Larry, for the hours of work and your gracious way of making so many of the books we've written far better and clearer. While you labor behind the scenes, you have blessed literally millions of homes over the years in your God-honoring career. Well done, good and faithful servant and friend.

Notes

CHAPTER 1 | IN SEARCH OF THE BLESSING

1. After reading this book, if you want to go deeper into the original works on the Blessing, here are two suggestions: *The Blessing* by John Trent, Ph.D., Gary Smalley, and Kari Trent Stageberg (Thomas Nelson, 2019) and the more recent abridgment, *The Power of the Blessing* by John Trent, Ph.D., and Gary Smalley with an introduction by Kari Trent Stageberg (Thomas Nelson, 2024).

CHAPTER 3 | WHY IT HURTS SO MUCH TO MISS THE BLESSING

1. Edward Tronick et al., "The Infant's Response to Entrapment between Contradictory Messages in Face-to-Face Interaction," *Journal of the American Academy of Child Psychiatry* 17, no. 1 (1978): 1–13, https://pubmed.ncbi.nlm.nih.gov/632477; "The 'Still-Face' Face Experiment by Dr. Ed Tronick," posted July 11, 2022, by UMass Chan Psychiatry and Behavioral Sciences, YouTube, 1 min., 54 sec., https://www.youtube.com/watch?v=FaiXi8KyzOQ.
2. *Steve! (Martin): A Documentary in 2 Pieces*, directed by Morgan Neville, released March 29, 2024, on Apple TV+.
3. Jim Wilder and Michel Hendricks, *The Other Half of Church: Christian Community, Brain Science, and Overcoming Spiritual Stagnation* (Moody, 2020), 19, emphasis added.

CHAPTER 5 | WHEN WE MISS THE SECOND ELEMENT: SPOKEN WORDS

1. *Pooh's Grand Adventure: The Search for Christopher Robin*, directed by Karl Geurs (Walt Disney Studios Home Entertainment, 1997).
2. "The Greatest Man I Never Knew," track 8 on Reba McEntire, *For My Broken Heart*, MCA, 1991.

3. See John Trent, "4 Animals Personality Test," Focus on the Family, March 11, 2024, https://www.focusonthefamily.com/marriage/4-animals -personality-test. For more, see John Trent, Ph.D., and Gary Smalley, *The Two Sides of Love: The Secret to Valuing Differences* (Tyndale House Publishers, 2019).

CHAPTER 6 | WHEN WE MISS THE THIRD ELEMENT: ATTACHING HIGH VALUE

1. "Inflation Calculator," accessed February 10, 2025, https://www .amortization.org/inflation.
2. Steve Martin, *Born Standing Up: A Comic's Life* (Scribner, 2007), 193.
3. Max Rieper, "'Brett' Documentary Reveals How a Complicated Father/Son Relationship Fueled a Hall of Fame Career," SB Nation, Royals Review, December 7, 2023, https://www.royalsreview.com/2023/12/7/23991640 /george-brett-documentary-mlb-network.

CHAPTER 8 | WHEN WE MISS THE FIFTH ELEMENT: GENUINE COMMITMENT

1. Julia Moore, "Jay Leno Tears Up as He Speaks about Wife Mavis amid Her Dementia Diagnosis: 'I Couldn't Be Prouder of Her,'" *People*, May 17, 2024, https://people.com/jay-leno-tears-up-speaking-about-wife-mavis -amid-dementia-diagnosis-8650313. Emphasis added.

CHAPTER 9 | HOMES THAT WITHHOLD THE BLESSING

1. Yang Claire Yang et al., "Social Relationships and Physiological Determinants of Longevity across the Human Life Span," *Proceedings of the National Academy of Sciences of the United States of America* 113, no. 3 (2016): 578–83, https://pmc.ncbi.nlm.nih.gov/articles/PMC4725506.
2. Krystine I. Batcho, "What Will Your Children Remember about You?" *Psychology Today*, June 18, 2015 https://www.psychologytoday.com/us /blog/longing-for-nostalgia/201506/what-will-your-children-remember -about-you.
3. Brie Turns-Coe, *Parent the Child You Have, Not the Child You Were: Break Generational Patterns. Raise Thriving Kids.* (PESI Publishing, 2023).
4. Quoted by Roger Hawley, "The Family Blessing: Implications for Counseling," unpublished paper, Texas Council of Family Relations Conference, 1983, Fort Worth, Texas.
5. "Gamblers More Likely to Have Suffered Childhood Traumas, Research Shows," University of Lincoln, August 2, 2017, https://news.lincoln .ac.uk/2017/08/02/gamblers-more-likely-to-have-suffered-childhood -traumas-research-shows.

CHAPTER 10 | "IT'S YOUR DAD"

1. *Field of Dreams*, directed by Phil Alden Robinson (Universal Pictures, 1989).

CHAPTER 11 | OUT OF CONTROL
1. Frederick Buechner, *Telling Secrets* (HarperCollins, 1991), 7–9.

CHAPTER 12 | THE MOMENT JESUS BROKE IN
1. Jerry Sittser, *A Grace Disguised: How the Soul Grows through Loss* (Zondervan, 1996).

CHAPTER 13 | CHOOSING TO CHANGE
1. Daniel Taylor, *The Healing Power of Stories: Creating Yourself through the Stories of Your Life* (Doubleday, 1996), 1–2.

CHAPTER 14 | WHEN YOU NEED TO SWITCH FATHERS
1. Leon Wood, *A Survey of Israel's History* (Zondervan, 1970), 366.

CHAPTER 17 | THE BEGINNING OF THE END OF YOUR WAR
1. "U.S. Military Casualties: Vietnam Conflict Casualty Summary," Defense Casualty Analysis System, as of February 4, 2025, https://dcas.dmdc.osd .mil/dcas/app/conflictCasualties/vietnam/vietnamSum.
2. Brent Ashabranner, *Always to Remember: The Story of the Vietnam Veterans Memorial* (Dodd, Mead, 1988), 66.
3. Quoted in Jan Scruggs, *The Wall That Heals* (Doubleday, 1992).
4. You can take this test at John Trent, Ph.D., "4 Animals Personality Test," Focus on the Family, March 11, 2024, https://www.focusonthefamily. com/marriage/4-animals-personality-test. For more, see John Trent, Ph.D., and Gary Smalley, *The Two Sides of Love: The Secret to Valuing Differences* (Tyndale House Publishers, 2019).
5. Abraham Lincoln, "Second Inaugural Address of the Late President Lincoln," Alfred Whital Stern Collection of Lincolniana, and Printed Ephemera Collection (James Miller, 1865), pdf, https://www.loc.gov/item /2020770559.

CHAPTER 19 | SO KEEP LOOKING DOWN!
1. Gerald Sittser, *A Grace Disguised: How the Soul Grows through Loss* (Zondervan, 1996), 50.

CHAPTER 20 | HOW GOD'S *BEING THERE* CAN HELP YOU BUILD LOVING ATTACHMENT
1. Sue Johnson with Kenny Sanderfer, *Created for Connection: The "Hold Me Tight" Guide for Christian Couples*, rev. ed. (Little, Brown, 2016), 56.
2. Adapted from Johnson with Sanderfer, *Created for Connection.*
3. Henri J. M. Nouwen, *You Are the Beloved: Daily Meditations for Spiritual Living*, ed. Gabrielle Earnshaw (Convergent Books, 2017), 97.
4. Max Lucado, *God Thinks You're Wonderful!* (Thomas Nelson, 2003), 13.

CHAPTER 21 | PREPARING FOR THE DAY THE DREAM OF A BLESSING ENDS

1. *Field of Dreams*, directed by Phil Alden Robinson (Universal Pictures, 1989).

CHAPTER 22 | STANDING STARTS ON YOUR KNEES

1. C. S. Lewis, *Letters to Malcolm: Chiefly on Prayer* (Harcourt, Brace, 1992), 16–18.

CHAPTER 24 | A MONTHLONG JOURNEY FROM MISSING TO RECEIVING, GIVING, AND LIVING THE BLESSING

1. David, "Did You Ever Fail, Lord?," in Norman C. Habel, *For Mature Adults Only* (Fortress Press, 1970), 28–29.
2. Linda Eyre and Richard Eyre, *Teaching Your Children Sensitivity* (Simon and Schuster, 1995), 92.
3. C. S. Lewis, *The Collected Letters of C. S. Lewis, vol. 3, Narnia, Cambridge and Joy 1950–1963*, ed. Walter Hooper (HarperSanFrancisco, 2007), 1438.
4. Frederick Buechner, *The Wizard's Tide: A Story* (HarperSanFrancisco, 1990), 44–46.
5. Lucille Burrascano, quoted in Marvin Heiferman and Carole Kismaric, *Talking Pictures: People Speak about the Photographs That Speak to Them* (Chronicle Books, 1994), 84–87.
6. John Kotre, *White Gloves: How We Create Ourselves through Memory* (W. W. Norton, 1996), 100–101.
7. Marjorie Holmes, "Teach Me to Talk to Them," in *Who Am I, God?* (Bantam Books, 1973), 15–16.
8. See Bruce Larson, *The One and Only You* (Word Books, 1974), 84–85.
9. Adapted from W. Livingston Larned, "Father Forgets," originally published in *People's Home Journal* 43, no. 4 (April 1928), 3.
10. Kotre, *White Gloves*, 101–102.
11. Mary Steichen Calderone, quoted in Heiferman and Kismaric, *Talking Pictures*, 206.
12. Mary Bahr Fritts, *The Memory Box*, illustrated by David Cunningham (Albert Whitman, 1992).

Inbox. *In sync.*

Focus on the Family's age & stage emails have specific content for your child's development right now. So you can spend more time being the intentional parent you want to be.

Visit
MyKidsAge.com
to learn more!

FOCUS ON THE FAMILY.

Stop playing it safe

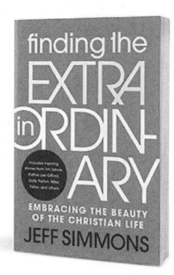

Step out, surpass the ordinary, and start living an *extraordinary* life for Christ.

Be inspired through the stories of people living extraordinary lives. Learn how you can live out God's plan for loving others, invest wisely in the things that matter, choose joy and share that joy freely with the world, discover your passion and purpose, and start living every day with motivation and meaning.

Scan here for the book.